D0923567

This new series of art and craft handbooks gives beginning students and amateurs enjoyable, practical introductions to a variety of creative activities. Each book, written by a leading artist or teacher, presents basic principles and includes specific instructions with step-by-step demonstrations.

Starting to Paint Portraits   Bernard Dunstan
Simple Toymaking   Sheila Jackson
Simple Pottery   Kenneth Drake
Pastels for Beginners   Ernest Savage
Starting to Paint in Oils   John Raynes
Making Mobiles   Anne & Christopher Moorey
Simple Printmaking   Cyril Kent and Mary Cooper
Starting with Watercolor   Rowland Hilder
Simple Jewelry   R.W. Stevens
Making Mosaics   John Berry
Bookbinding for Beginners   John Corderoy
Woodcarving for Beginners   Charles Graveney
Making Posters   Vernon Mills
Making Soft Toys   Gillian Lockwood

These **Watson-Guptill Art and Craft Handbooks**
are now available to schools and libraries in
GOLDENCRAFT BINDING
From GOLDEN PRESS, INC., Educational Division
and its regular distributors.
850 Third Ave., New York, N.Y. 10022

Bookbinding for Beginners

Bookbinding for Beginners

John Corderoy

with line illustrations
by Eric Sweet

Studio Vista   London

Watson-Guptill Publications   New York

Cover:
Decoration of this kind can be drawn on a cover: lettering with transfer
is simple after a little practice. The blue book is from The First Edition
Club, 1930; the others are the work of students at art schools in Cam-
berwell, Oxford and Maidstone.

General Editor Jean Richardson
© John Corderoy 1967
Published in London by Studio Vista Limited
Blue Star House, Highgate Hill, London N 19
and in New York by Watson-Guptill Publications
165 West 46th Street, New York 10036
Distributed in Canada by General Publishing Co. Ltd.
30 Lesmill Road, Don Mills, Toronto, Canada
Library of Congress Catalog Card Number 67-13739
Set in Folio Grotesque 8 and 9 pt.
Printed in the Netherlands
by N.V. Grafische Industrie Haarlem

Contents

Introduction   7

1   Small tools   9
2   Special equipment   12
3   Materials   25
4   Paper   30
5   The first stage: folding, sewing, endpapers   37
6   The second stage: gluing, edge-cutting, the spine   42
7   The third stage: casing and finishing   50
8   Rebinding a book   60
9   Unsewn binding   65
10   Sewing unsewn books   71
11   Library binding in leather   77
12   Decoration   94
13   Repairing cloth covers   99
For further reading   102
List of suppliers   103
Index   104

Der Buchbinder.

Introduction

You can start bookbinding on the kitchen table with the simplest equipment and a few easily obtained materials. You need each of the following: pocket-knife, scissors, bone paper-knife, needle, paint-brush, hammer, steel rule, and four drawing-pins or thumb tacks; flour paste and glue, or PVA adhesive, airmail paper, drawing paper, cereal packets, thread, tape, some bookcloth or very strong paper, letter transfers to make titles, and a newspaper to save having to clean the table when you've finished. A pile of books or a racket-press will be useful to hold things flat.

This is a rather basic approach, so I've taken a more sophisticated view and described the proper tools and materials first; and then suggested substitutes.

There's no mystery in bookbinding, and the only qualification is the urge to bind books. Anyone with sufficient interest can invent a protective covering - it's been done for 1500 years, and it still goes on - but there are fewer disappointments if you can draw on previous experience, and this book is intended as a guide to beginners.

The working space and equipment that you need must be regulated to suit available resources and should be added to gradually. Collecting tools, in case they may be useful, is expensive and inefficient.

Some of the best bindings of recent years were done in a room twelve feet square, which was also used for living and sleeping in, and with the simplest tools. It takes a lot of enthusiasm to work in so compact an environment. Schools and clubs provide guidance and the use of equipment, but the best place for leisure activity is at home. The meeting-place is worth while for the exchange of ideas, and a bookbinder is always anxious to explain - in the friendliest way - the advantages of doing it his way. The bookbinders in Jost Amman's woodcut opposite would soon be at home in a modern hand bindery, as the tools are still similar to those of 1568. They might be surprised at the number of books and our casual acceptance of them, and to know that every bookbinder can read.

Woodcut of bookbinders by Jost Amman from *Eygentliche Beschreibung aller Stände auff Erden*, 1568. (British Museum)

7

There is a correct sequence of operations when doing any job - it develops as a matter of expediency - and success depends on proper design, not chance.

Design has been defined as 'the preliminary conception of an idea that is to be carried into effect by action', and it is a good idea to have some notion of what you intend doing before starting. Too many people think of design as a pretty, decorative treatment - but that's only the most apparent part of it.

A good design for a book takes into account its function, probable period of life, the kind of use it may expect, its size, its price, and appearance.

You, as a bookbinder, are not likely to have any choice in the type used in printing, the size, or the paper used - though many bookbinders think they could have done better - but all other decisions are yours.

You will have to decide how the book is to be sewn, what endpapers to use, the construction of the binding, covering materials (which include colour, texture, and finish) and the decoration of the cover. If these are worked out beforehand, you will know what to do next and can have materials ready for the next process - and you won't find yourself saying 'If I'd only thought of that earlier . . .'

It needs experience to make these decisions, but this accumulates; as it does, you will find that pre-planning, design, whatever you care to call it, will pay off well. Know what you intend doing - and why.

In the early stages you must concentrate on using traditional methods and materials in order to do clean, neat work. This will give understanding of materials and confidence in your skill. The next step is to try something different (but remember that there is no virtue in difference for its own sake). If it goes wrong you may discover why - and that's good. Be shameless and copy the work of others; they may be flattered, or think you stupidly ambitious, or give you help and guidance. All the time, whenever you handle a book, use your special knowledge to analyse it and think of how and why it was done - and how it could be improved. Remember that nothing is perfect, and treasure your dissatisfaction.

Thanks to Sally Lou Smith, who read and corrected in many stages, and Eric Sweet, who made comments with his drawings, some of the imperfections have been removed from this book.

1 Small tools

Boards: there are many kinds, but two will suffice here. Backing boards, made from beech, are 5" wide and have one edge $\frac{1}{2}$" wide and rounded to avoid marking the book, and the other edge $\frac{5}{8}$" wide and bevelled to give an edge with a 75° angle, over which the sections are turned when a book is being backed. The edge will need to be planed if it becomes bruised or broken.

Pressing boards may be made from 10 mm plywood, or they can be made up by cutting millboard to size and gluing a number of thicknesses together. The sizes are governed by the sizes of presses and books.

Bodkin: sold as marking awls or garnish awls. Used for spiking holes in boards and paper.

Brushes: for glue, should be as large as will fit easily in your gluepot; they should be round and have long bristles.

Paste brushes are similar, but must be string-bound or have aluminium ferrules to avoid rust. These brushes are also suitable for PVA adhesive.

Small paint brushes can be useful at times.

Soak brushes well before using them for the first time, and keep them moist or the bristles will become loose.

Dividers: 6" spring dividers with a screw adjustment.

Drill brace: an ordinary hand-drill.

Folder: bone folding-sticks about 8" x 1" x $\frac{1}{8}$" with round or pointed ends. They are used for folding paper, rubbing down glued materials to make them stick, turning in edges, in fact all the time. Have several, and shape them to your needs. If soaked in oil for a day and then washed, they are easy to keep clean.

Files: for tool-making. Almost any file will be useful, but sharp, new ones save a lot of work. Always keep a file in a handle - the pointed tang in your hand can be quite painful. Small 'Swiss' files are a great help.

Gold cushion: for use when laying out gold leaf. Make this from wood about 10" x 6" x $\frac{3}{4}$", with a $\frac{1}{4}$" layer of newspaper covered with rough calf which is turned down over the edges and tacked in position every inch. The leather must be tight. Any non-greasy leather will do. Keep it covered when not in use.

Gold knife: a knife with a blade about 8″ long and 1″ wide. The edge should be slightly rough to cut gold, but not sharp enough to cut the gold cushion. The only other use it has is paper-slitting. Keep it free of grease.

Hammer: a small size of shoemaker's hammer.

Knives: a good general purpose knife is the kind used by shoemakers - preferably without a wooden handle. The best knives are made from the discarded blades of power hacksaws: these can be ground on a carborundum wheel without doing significant damage to the steel. Wrap leather around them to save your hands; this can be pasted or glued.

Knives should be ground on the top side only - the under side must be flat. They are, therefore, left or right-handed.

Needles: the egg-eyed needles known as 'sharps' are best for hard thread. Sizes 1, 3 and 6 are enough.

Oil stones: coarse and fine India stones 8″ x 2″ x 1″.

Paring stone: smooth (calcium carbonate) stones, formerly

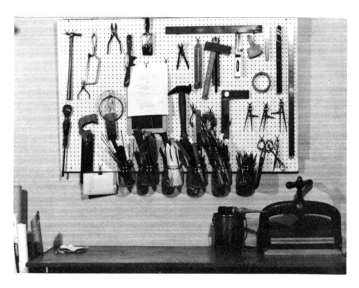

A pegboard over the work-bench will hold tools easily - this one is in regular use. The bench under it is made from a pair of crates and a blockboard panel.

used by lithographers, are used for most leather work as they are smooth and form a good working surface. A marble wash-stand top or a looking-glass with a polished edge will serve.

Pin-vice: a small hand-tool with a drill-chuck head that will hold a needle when piercing thick papers.

Plane: a No. 4 plane is ideal, but any general purpose plane will do.

Punch: for making clean round holes, use a round-hole punch with a hammer; $\frac{1}{4}''$ diameter is most useful.

Saw: an old back-saw with blunt teeth, or a hacksaw. The little bent-wire saws with narrow blades are handy.

Shears: heavy scissors, about $8\frac{1}{4}''$.

Sponge: natural or synthetic sponges for damping and washing paper, cloth, and leather.

Square: an 8″ carpenter's square. Check it to make sure it is true against the straight edge of a board: draw a line, turn the square over, and draw another to find if they coincide. Squares are often not true.

Straight-edge: a piece of $1\frac{1}{4}''$ x $\frac{1}{8}''$ bright mild steel 15″ long, to use as a guide when cutting straight with a knife. Thin rules are unsafe.

Strop: 15″ x 2″ plywood with 12″ of leather glued on and dressed with a little oil and jeweller's rouge.

Tins: tinned iron plates, about .020″ thick, with paper folded over them, are put inside the boards when books are being pressed to save marking the book. Alclad or Duralumin sheet is sometimes used.

Twist drill bits: will be useful if you do any toolcutting. Number drills give a better choice of sizes.

Vice: a small vice that can be clamped to the bench is often useful - it leaves both hands free.

Weights: lead weights will be constantly useful. They can be cast in a millboard box 4″ x 3″ x 1″, with a wire around the walls to stop it from falling apart. Have a stone floor under the mould. Any weight will do - an old flat-iron if you still have one.

Zinc plate: about .030″ thick (English Zinc Gauge 14 or Standard Wire Gauge 21) to use under material that is being cut with a knife and straight-edge. Zinc, being soft, will not blunt the knife. Useful sizes are 12″ x 4″ and 18″ x 12″.

2 Special equipment

The bookbinding trade uses a great variety of machines for mass production of books, but the essentials are very simple: even these can be scaled down to suit the means available to someone who wants to bind books at home.

The bench

As most bookbinding is done in a standing position, the height of a bench is important. The standard height is 36″, but you yourself may not be a standard size, so try to have the working level about 3″ below the top of your hip-bone and be comfortable. The ideal workbench would be 10 yards long! If you get 10 feet you will be fortunate, and if it is covered with thick linoleum, doubly so.

Electric and gas outlets are valuable, and a good light essential, but if there is direct sunlight, use a white curtain to diffuse the light. A supply of water should be reasonably near.

Try to keep the bench-top clear, except for a small press, a zinc plate for cutting on, the glue-pot and its heater, and

a pot of paste. A pegboard on the wall will keep many tools easily available, and glass jars will hold bone folders, small brushes, knives, and all the long thin bits and pieces that are inevitable and indispensible. There are special jar-clips that fit on pegboard.

Beneath the bench is a fine place for the size of shelf that is needed to store paper and boards. It need not be solid, as the paper is likely to be kept in large folders that can be supported by three or four rails running from back to front of the bench frame. Think, also, of the smaller things needing shelf space and try to find a place for them at the end of the bench: remember that you may want to sit, so leave a space to allow for this. A seat should be 10″ lower than the surface of the bench.

This is all very pleasant in theory - you'll probably use the kitchen table anyhow.

In the foreground of Jost Amman's woodcut (see frontis-piece), the bookbinder is using a plough (plow) to cut a book in the press that is lying against his knees. In the background, another man is sewing a book on a sewing-frame. These are special tools that have hardly changed since those times, and you will need something to hold your work.

The lying-press

This consists of two jaws, or cheeks, made of beech or some other smooth, tough hardwood. Two screws of the same timber are traditional, but steel screws give more power and are less prone to distortion - the screws are made fast in one cheek and threaded into the other; two square guide-bars keep the faces level, and, if the press is to be used for edge-cutting, one cheek will have a pair of rails for the plough to run in. The press rests on a stand or 'tub', but it can be let into a bench and covered when not in use. It is, however, so constantly in use that the cover may not be needed.

A useful substitute for the lying-press can be made with two lengths of 2″ x 3″ planed beech with a 1″-diameter bench screw at each end. The timber will need stiffening with an angle-iron to prevent it from bending too much when pressure is applied. This will serve all purposes except cutting with a plough, and could still be useful if you ever acquired a more normal tool. When you do get a press, it should have 18″ to 24″ between the screws, each cheek should be 5″ wide by about 3½″ deep, and their inside, upper, and lower surfaces must be smooth and true. The upper and lower surfaces of the guide rails must be a running fit, or the press will not close accurately. If wooden screws are fitted, they must be free of distortion and smoothly finished.

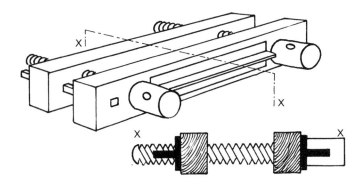

The plough (plow)

This is a tool for cutting the edges of books and boards with great accuracy. It was largely replaced by the guillotine in the mid-19th century, but many bookbinders contend that the plough still produces a better edge.

The plough has many points in common with the lying-press - two cheeks, two guide bars, but only one screw to control the distance between the cheeks.

The left cheek fits in the guides on the lying-press and has the screw threaded into it; the right cheek holds the screw (but allows it to turn) with its handle projecting on the right-hand side, and has the plough-knife held horizontally in its base with the edge of the blade just clearing the press surface. A screw with a dovetail groove in one end holds the blade against two metal plates let into the sides of the right-hand cheek. The blade has a dovetail section to fit into the groove, and it is impossible to overstate the need for keeping the edge very sharp and the underside absolutely flat. If you can, get a blade made of Stellite (a special alloy steel that keeps a good edge).

The lack of a plough will not deter anyone who really wants to bind books: very good edges have been cut with the book held in press and no other equipment than a very sharp paring chisel. The enthusiast will always improvise.

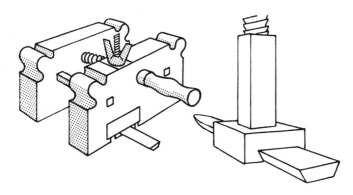

The millboard cutter

This is a heavy piece of equipment that is hardly mentioned in this book because you are unlikely to get one: but it is the best tool for cutting boards, and the tool most frequently missed by amateurs who know about it. There are small table models, but they are rarely capable of holding a board steadily as it is being cut. Don't be misled into thinking that a photographic print-trimmer will do.

A proper machine will cut a 30″ board of ⅛″ thickness; it has an iron table with a straight gauge along one side at right-angles to the blade, which is fixed to the long edge; a sliding gauge runs parallel to the cutting edge. At the far end of the table, another blade is pivoted so that it can be pulled down beside the fixed one, shearing as it goes. Slightly behind the cutting edge is a foot-operated clamp to hold the board with an even pressure along its whole length.

When using this machine, cut boards a little larger than is necessary, with one good long edge; lay the good edge against the side and square one end of each board; mark the desired length on one board, set the sliding gauge to this mark, and cut the other end of each board. Re-set the sliding gauge, cut the width, and all the boards should be the same size with each corner a right angle. When cutting several boards, always put them down in the same way after cutting: never turn one board - always the whole stack.

This looks a dangerous machine, but a pinched finger is the commonest accident.

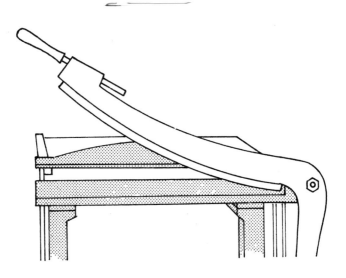

The cutting clamp

This is a tool to make, or have made, from easily obtained materials. It can be used to hold work steady when thin books and boards are being cut with a sharp knife, in the absence of a plough and press.

A plywood base (A) 16″ - or longer - by 8″ by 1″ thick, has two 3/8″ holes drilled through it; the holes are 1″ from each end, and 2″ from the working edge. Two lengths of

Bound by Sally Lou Smith in her fifth year of bookbinding. Courtesy of the Victoria & Albert Museum.

Decoration using random lines or two colours of fabric.

A few simple tools are all you need to start bookbinding: others can follow if you want to do more advanced work.

The plough and lying-press are traditional tools for cutting the edges of books. A linen-press can be used for pressing books.

1″ outside diameter pipe (B), with the ends plugged, are drilled to match the holes in the base. Two ⅜″ by 6″ bolts (C) pass through one pipe and the base, and light compression springs (D) are fitted over them; the second pipe goes over the springs, and wing-nuts (E) hold the pipe down.

A ¾″ by 2″ hardwood straight-edge (F) with a ¾″ wide steel strip screwed (countersunk) to one edge, fits between the screws and rests on the work; the wing-nuts provide pressure, and a knife with a flat underside is used to make a series of cuts. A zinc plate under the work will protect the base and ensure clean final cuts.

When this tool is in use, the lower pipe must be off the end of the bench to help hold it steady - in fact, you could keep it screwed in position permanently if there is room to do so.

Countersunk screws, to be tightened with a screwdriver, necessitate threading the lower pipe; but they leave a clearer run along the top pipe.

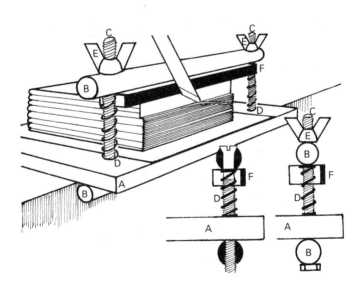

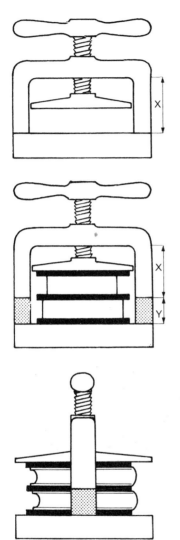

Nipping presses

The need to press books often, and for long periods, has made bookbinders press-conscious. Their variety is remarkable but all they do is hold books flat under pressure. The old-fashioned linen press does as much if the timbers are not distorted, but an iron press is better. The copying press, which used to be common office furniture, is quite useful, but the 'daylight' or height from base to platen (x) is too small. This can be increased by removing the screws that hold the base to the arch and replacing them with longer ones. The extra two or three inches must be made up with blocks of hardwood or lengths of iron pipe (y): the platen will no longer meet the base, but pressing-boards and books can fill the gap.

You will need pressing-boards made of prime grade 10 mm plywood. Have some as large as the press will hold with ease, for large books; and some smaller ones for more usual sizes. The edges should be smoothly finished but not rounded.

When pressing books, always make sure that the centre of the book is under the screw.

The sewing-frame

This is another wooden tool that is peculiar to bookbinders. A baseboard with a slot near the front edge is raised from the bench by a batten at each end; the front edge is bevelled as far as the slot to make sewing easier. Screw-threaded posts have wooden nuts to raise or lower a crossbar. Tape or cord fastened to the crossbar is held below the slot by sewing keys, and is made taut by pushing up the bar with the screw nuts. Sewing-frames vary in length from 12″ to 36″ or more.

This is one of the simplest tools to improvise. The traditional frame is a bulky, but decorative, object: you may find it convenient to make one that folds down when it isn't in use. A baseboard and front rail screwed to a pair of battens, with two uprights and a crossbar made as a separate unit and attached by a screw at each end, will fold down for storage without taking off partly sewn work. Tension for the tapes or cords is provided by strong elastic bands kept on the crossbar for that purpose.

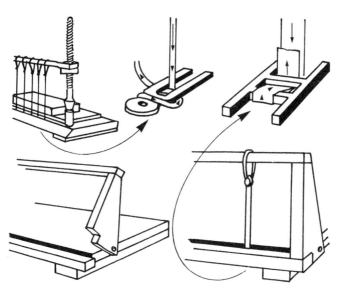

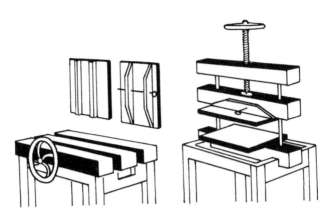

Combination presses

Inventive minds will always devise tools that will do more than one job. In France, where there are many amateur bookbinders, a popular model of lying-press can be turned on its side to be used as a nipping-press: unfortunately, you can't use it both ways at once. It is a very nice tool if you can get one.

Another interesting idea that appeals to beginners - especially where price is concerned - is a small press that can be used for pressing books, backing, and for cutting edges with a sharp knife. The Digby Stuart press (in U.S. the Portable Book Press from Technical Library Service) does not pretend to be a tool for advanced workers, but it gives large classes of young pupils, and people who work at home, the chance to start bookbinding.

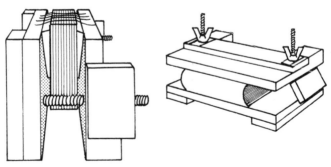

The finishing stove

This heater for the tools and letters that are used when putting titles and decoration on books is usually circular, so that the tools can be heated in the centre, while the handles are supported by a gallery in a position that keeps them cool. It can be heated electrically, but oil or gas can be more easily controlled.

Finishing stoves may be bought ready-made, but the demand is small and it can be cheaper to have one made, from $\frac{1}{4}''$ iron wire, by a blacksmith. The whole thing centres on a gas burner (A) over which a metal plate (B), about twice the diameter of the burner, acts as a heat deflector; a circular support (C), for the tools, should be 1" to $1\frac{1}{2}''$ away from the plate and, 5" away from that, another ring (G) supports the wooden handles; if the outside ring has a wave form every two inches, it will help to locate the tools. These three units are joined by three radial rods (E). Three V-shaped legs, welded to the outside ring, should be tall enough to hold the deflector plate 2" above the burner: you can decide on their height after getting the burner.

If you decide on an electric stove, choose one with a quick-boiling element and a simmerstat switch: the solid hotplate type is most frustrating when there is not sufficient contact between the tool and the plate for an adequate transfer of heat.

Any of these stoves can be used as a glue-pot heater.

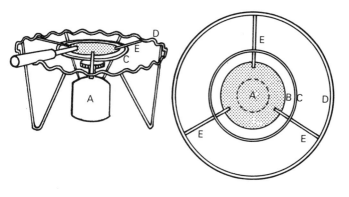

The type-clamp

This is a tool to enable you to use single pieces of type
when it is inconvenient to work with a type-holder in which
a line of type is set; it works on the same principle as a
toolmaker's cramp. The lower screw is used to adjust the
width of the jaws; the upper one presses them apart at one
end to provide a grip at the tip of the tool. The distance from
the lower screw to the tip is ¾″, to let the typeface stand
clear. If made in brass, this tool will hold heat well. (See
section on finishing, page 55.)

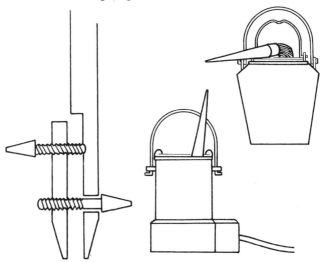

The glue-pot

This is in two parts: a cast-iron glue container in a water-
jacket - a double-boiler, in fact. A modern version has an
electric heater built into the water-jacket. A thermostatically
controlled electric heater is the best: it is safe to leave it on
for a week without damaging the glue or the brush. This pot
has no water-jacket to become foul if it is left for any
length of time.

   When not in use, the glue brush should rest on the scraping
wire across the top of the glue container.

3 Materials

Bank paper: see Paper.

Blocking foil: thin plastic film with a high-vacuum deposit of gold or other metal backed by heat-sensitive adhesive; non-metallic coloured foils are also made. Reels are of various lengths; width of reel is optional and price is reckoned by width of reel.

Writing foil is similar, but has a pressure-sensitive adhesive.

Boards: those for making book covers are made from waste paper, straw, and other papermaking materials. Better grades of waste paper are used for millboards (originally made from cordage and old nets and called binder's board in the USA) which are found in better types of binding. These are best for your work. Two thicknesses, .040″ and .056″, can be glued together in various combinations to give the range 40, 56, 80, 96, 112 thousandths of an inch, which will cover most of your needs. In the USA pasteboard is a less expensive substitute for binder's board. Rough-cut them ½″ larger all round than you need, glue them together, and trim to size after they have been pressed.

Strawboard, from Holland, is made from macerated straw and tends to brittleness. It is yellow in colour.

Chipboard, often called Thames board, is made from all grades of waste paper. It is often lined on one or both sides with kraft fibre which may be the outer ply of the board. It bends and creases well.

The most convenient sizes for boards are 20″ x 25″ and 25″ x 30″; they are sold in bundles of 56 lb. It is practical to use even cereal packets (chipboard) if the grain is right and the printing has made no dents. Most cartons are chipboard.

Bookcloth: a stiffened, usually cotton, fabric with a filling or lining to prevent glue penetration. Colour may be due to dying or surface treatment; and it may be washable and fadeless, or either. Blues, greys and greens were prone to fading.

The names by which cloths are known can be misleading - art vellum, art canvas, buckram - so choose those that look like woven material and avoid any that are made to look otherwise: most embossed cloths are weakened.

There are many cloths with cellulose nitrate or PVC coatings on one side which are described as leathercloth because they have a leather grain embossing. They are useful for workshop and kitchen books as they can be washed - the smoother grains collect less dirt.

Paper with a PVC coating is also available - the PVC wears very well, but the paper will break if strained. Bookcloth is often made in rolls 38″ to 40″ wide; the usual length of a roll is 40 yards, so you will need a supplier who will let you have cut lengths.

Carbon tetrachloride (Carbona): usually abbreviated to CTC. A non inflammable, heavy (SG 1.6), volatile liquid. Useful as a solvent and grease remover.

WARNING: CTC gives off a harmful gas (chlorine) which, when passed over charcoal - a cigarette produces charcoal - turns to phosgene, a more harmful gas.

Cartridge paper: a common description for a wide range of printing and drawing papers with unglazed surfaces. Useful for endpapers if they are strong enough.

Scotch tape or Cellotape: a self-adhesive transparent plastic tape. It can be removed by CTC which dissolves the adhesive. Keep it in a container or it will shrink and the centre will rise to a cone.

Cellulose varnish: usually available in an aerosol dispenser. Useful as a protective sealing film if it is used in moderation. Inflammable! Use it in a free current of air, and don't let it get into your eyes.

Cord: hemp cord is used for book-sewing, but is not mentioned in the text. If cord has been used on books to be repaired, do not replace with tape; use hemp or nylon cord.

Cow gum: see Rubber solution.

Drawing pins: also called thumb-tacks.

Foil: see Blocking foil.

Glaire, glair: an adhesive for gold leaf. A stock can be made by soaking 1 oz flake albumen in 10 oz water until the flake has dissolved, straining the liquid through cotton wool, and adding 1/20th oz phenol as a preservative. There are many versions of this - see page 91 for another.

Some modern substitutes are considered excellent, but each binder makes his own decision.

Glue: a hot adhesive that sets as it cools; a crude form of gelatine. Cabinet-maker's glue in pearl or sugar form should be soaked overnight to make it swell - 5 oz glue to 10 oz

water. This can be done in the glue-pot that is to contain it.
  Heat above 150° F. will spoil glue: 120° to 130° is adequate. Heat the glue occasionally, even if you don't want to use it, to prevent mould formation.

Gold foil: see Blocking foil.

Gold leaf: gold (about 23 carat) beaten to a thickness of, roughly, .000004″. Used for gold-tooling on leather and for edge-gilding. Gold blocking foil has largely superseded it, but it is still used on the best work. It is sold in books of 25 leaves 3¼″ square.

Gold rubber: pure rubber soaked in turpentine and left until it is no longer gummy, is used to remove and collect surplus gold from surfaces that have been tooled. The gold can be refined.

Kraft paper: strong paper used for wrapping. True kraft paper leaves a small quantity of very soft ash if it is burned - this indicates a very pure form of cellulose fibre. Use it where strength is the prime consideration - linings of spines, some endpapers. Kraft is made in a variety of colours, but the usual one is the natural brown: there are bleached varieties. Long, strong, chemical wood fibres are used for making this paper.

Leather: bookbinding leather is usually vegetable tanned. It should be supple, have a firm texture, and the colour should not fade or shift very much when wet. Goatskin, often called morocco, is most useful; some pigskin is good; calf is weak and expensive - it has a very smooth surface that shows every mark; sheepskin is cheap, but the surface is soft and the inner and outer layers of the skin tend to separate.
  Colour is influenced by the original pink-buff of vegetable-tanned leathers: white and pastel tints can only be produced by spraying with cellulose-bound pigments. These render the surface water-resistant, it is difficult to make gold stick, and the skins are no longer suitable for bookbinding. The nearest colour to white is obtained by alum-tawing, which produces an extremely durable ivory-coloured skin that gets darker as the years go on.

Manilla card: an extremely tough card, usually glazed, much used in filing systems.

Millboard: see Boards.

Mull: a stiffened cotton material having an open weave. Used for lining the spines of books.

Paper: see chapter 4 for description and properties. Paper is sold by weight. In the UK there are many sizes with names that are traditional:

foolscap 13½" x 17"	large post 16½" x 21"
crown 15" x 20"	medium 18" x 23"
demy 17½" x 22½"	imperial 22" x 30"
royal 20" x 25"	

Most of these may be had in double sizes (double the short edge) or quad sizes (double both edges). A paper made in the seven basic sizes and in four different thicknesses will make reams (500 sheets) of twenty-eight different weights. The continental system is to weigh a sheet of paper one metre square and give the weight in grammes per square metre (gsm): four descriptions instead of twenty-eight. In this book, all descriptions are in gsm as it has become the international method. The 'substance' of the paper on which this book is printed is about 100 gsm: but a softer paper of the same thickness would be less, and a glossy magazine paper more.

Unless you buy paper by the ream, you will have to rely on printers or merchants willing to sell small lots. If you are not sure that a particular paper will do what you expect of it, the merchant who sells it will usually give a sample sheet to try.

Try to have a small stock of:

Acid-free tissue or, better, fine Japanese tissue, for mending damaged sheets.

Airmail paper 16½" x 21", 30 gsm: rag content if you can get it. For mending and guarding sections.

Bank paper 16½" x 21", 45 gsm: for guarding sections, reinforcing weak papers and lining coloured end-papers.

Woodfree cartridge 20" x 25", 100 gsm: for endpapers and blank books.

Ribbed kraft paper, any size, 100 gsm: for endpapers, lining spines, and wrapping. The usual colour is brown, but there are others.

Manilla card 20½" x 30½", 225 gsm: for spines of cases and making split boards. Buff colour is best.

Paste: make this by mixing 3 oz plain flour and half a teaspoon of alum with enough water to make it creamy. Add sufficient water to make 20 oz, heat it to boiling point, and keep it there for five minutes. Stir constantly to avoid lumps. Stir frequently as it cools to prevent a skin from forming.

Add a piece of thymol, about the size of a pea, when the temperature is about 100° F. to prevent moulds from forming - crush the thymol. This paste keeps well in a jar with a loose lid.

Paste (corn starch): see chapter on rebinding a book.

PVA (polyvinyl acetate) emulsion adhesive: a thick, white adhesive which may be thinned with water, but will not dissolve in water after it has set. It remains soft but tough and appears to be an excellent adhesive for unsewn binding. It does not replace glue or paste.

Printers' ink: a very great range of colours may be mixed for tooling and decorating covers without the need for heating the tools. The ink must be cleaned from the tools with paraffin (kerosene).

Rubber solution: rubber solution in naphtha is a useful temporary adhesive that can be removed easily.

Tape: stiffened India tape is commonly used for sewing books, but any strong tape can be used, and stiffening with paste, thin glue, or starch will make sewing easier. Linen tape is very strong; nylon or terylene strongest. The width is not important, but $\frac{1}{2}''$ is the widest you should need.

Thread: used for sewing books. Unbleached linen thread with a glazed finish is usual, but nylon, terylene, cotton, and cotton with terylene are all used.

2-oz reels of linen in a range of thicknesses should be kept: 16-4 cord, 25-3 cord, 35-2 cord, and 50-2 cord will cover your needs.

If one pound of flax is spun to a length of 300 yards, its number is 1; if spun to 600 yards, No. 2; 900 yards, No. 3, and so on. No. 16 is 4800 yards, and 16-4 is made from four cords of No. 16. No. 50 is a strand of 15000 yards which, doubled, becomes 50-2 cord.

Cotton is worked on a similar principle: No. 1 is 840 yards.

4 Paper

Before you've done any bookbinding, you may think that paper is merely a flat, thin substance used for writing, printing, and wrapping parcels: you will find that it has a will of its own and can behave in a very lively manner. As paper is the foundation of bookbinding, it will be helpful to know some of its ways - for it can help you if you make it work for you.

Paper can be made from the structural cells of most flower-bearing plants - these are usually hollow, tiny, tubular in form, and range from about 1 to 25 millimetres in length; the walls are composed of cellulose, so they are referred to as cellulose fibres. Because plants grow in different ways, the cells are not all the same shape or size and some have been found more useful than others for papermaking.

Before papermaking begins, the raw materials are cut into small pieces and treated chemically to remove the unformed cellulose, sap, natural gums and resins which are of no use in paper: the preparation of 'groundwood' fibre for newsprint is an exception, and the impurities are, in part, responsible for its rapid deterioration. Only pure cellulose will make a stable paper.

Cotton and flax, in the form of rags, give good long fibres which make strong and durable papers, but the cost is high; spruce and pine supply the bulk of basic fibre in the northern hemisphere, and the chemical processes to which they are subjected give a wide range of stable papers for most purposes. When they are treated by the purely mechanical 'groundwood' process, the unstable, weak, bulky fibre needs reinforcement by 'chemical' wood to produce newsprint, in which permanence and strength are less important than low cost. Incidentally, the term 'woodfree' means free of groundwood. Esparto grass is used in Europe, where its short, fine fibres are used, with the addition of chemical wood or rag fibres, to make smooth white papers with good opacity.

The preparation of fibre for papermaking varies with the properties that the paper is to have, but the basic process of forming the sheet is always the same: a filter, usually of woven bronze wire, is used to separate the fibre from the water in which it is suspended. In primitive methods, the 'stuff' is poured on the filter; handmade paper is produced by sliding the filter into a vat and litfting it out with the fibres on the wire; machine-made paper comes from a moving woven wire belt passing under a shallow sluice through which the water and fibre flow - a reversion to the primitive method, but much faster.

When the web of paper leaves the wire part of the machine, it goes through felt-covered press rolls and a series of heated cylinders on which it is dried before being reeled up. The strength of the felted fibres is directly related to their length; you must always remember that paper is a large number of holes held together by these fibres and that they are tubular.

Machine-made is the only type we need consider, as the handmade method is almost finished. The stuff (1% fibre in 99% water) flows to a wire moving at 12 to 30 miles an hour, and the fibres tend to be drawn in the direction of travel; this produces a grain in the machine direction that will affect your work. These are the considerations:

(a) Cellulose fibre, in the form of flattened-tubes, tends to lie in one direction when paper is machine-made. This makes it easier to tear, fold, or bend along the grain: harder across.

(b) Tubes draw in moisture by capillary action - the finer the tube, the quicker the action. When flattened cellulose fibre draws in moisture, it expands more in width than length, so paper expands across the grain as it becomes wet: when the water evaporates, the fibre shrinks - and so does the paper.

Make sure that you understand this by testing all the paper that you use, and remember that boards (bookbinders never speak of 'cardboard') are only a thicker form of paper with the same physical properties.

(a) Take about twenty sheets of paper and bend them across the width, then across the length. One way will offer less resistance than the other, because you will be bending around the grain and not overcoming the stiffness of all those tubular fibres. Books made with the grain parallel to the spine open well: others do not, and will often cockle across the leaves.

(b) Tear a strip from the short edge of a sheet of paper and another from the long edge: one will tear more easily and straighter because the tear is along the grain and fewer fibres are being broken.

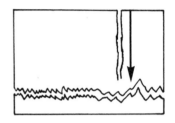

(c) Breathe on one side of the corner of a piece of paper, held about an inch (25 mm) from your mouth, and it will curl slightly; if you lay it on a damp surface, it will curl strongly because the fibres on one surface have expanded in width - the curl will be around the grain direction. As the moisture penetrates, the paper will flatten; shrinkage takes place as the moisture dries off.

(d) Fold a sheet of paper along and across the grain. The fold along the grain will be easier to make and will lie flatter: so will books made this way.

(e) Mark the grain direction on a sheet of paper, paste it to a piece of board and let it dry. Notice the effect, then do the same on the other side of the board but with the grain across that of the first sheet. This will give some idea of the power of the shrinking cellulose fibre.

Some treatment is needed to reduce moisture absorption by paper, unless it is to be used for blotting or filters. This can be done by 'tub-sizing' in a warm bath of 1% to 2% gelatine which seals the surface, gives smooth finish, protects the fibres, and adds strength. It is ideal for writing papers. Printing papers are 'engine-sized' with rosin which, when added to the pulp, precipitates on the fibres. This method is that in general use and it is so good that classification into writing, printing, and drawing paper is hardy needed and few users are aware that such divisions exist.

A rough test of tensile strength is useful. Hold a strip of paper between your thumbs and index fingers, with the tips of your thumbs touching; grip firmly, then press up with your thumbs to find how much force is needed to break the paper. Try again at right angles to the first test. You may find that some book-covering papers will not break - you may use them with confidence.

Take a new look at paper - find out if books have the grain along or across the spine. Are the leaves cockled? Do books open well and lie flat? But don't be too critical of books before 1800; there was no machine-made paper and the cockled leaves are due to the fact that the sheets were damped before printing and the type impression stretched the middle of each leaf - that kind of printing was done for a long time, even into the nineteenth century.

Sequence of operations:

a check list for New books in sheets
Rebinding case books
Library binding in leather

N	.	.	Fold sections
N	R	L	Collate
.	R	L	Pull
.	R	L	Mend torn leaves
.	R	L	Guard in plates
.	R	L	Guard sections
N	R	L	Press overnight, make endpapers
N	R	L	Mark for sewing
N	R	L	Sew, attach endpapers
N	R	L	Glue spine
N	R	L	Cut edges
N	R	L	Round, back
N	R	L	Clean off spine and leave in press to dry
N	R	.	Line spine with mull and paper
.	.	L	Make split boards
N	R	L	Cut boards to size
N	R	.	Cut stiffener for case
.	.	L	Attach boards to book
N	R	.	Make case
.	.	L	Cut out leather spine
.	.	L	Spokeshave leather
.	.	L	Cut out leather corners
.	.	L	Pare turn-ins of leather
.	.	L	Cover leather corners
.	.	L	Cover leather spine
.	.	L	Trim out sides
.	.	L	Fill in sides
.	.	L	Cut cloth sides to fit
.	.	L	Glue on sides
.	.	L	Trim margin of turn-in
N	R	L	Paste down endpapers and press
.	.	L	Mark and blind-tool bands if necessary
N	R	L	Make lettering pattern
.	.	L	Blind-tool lettering
.	.	L	Glair letter impressions (twice)
.	.	L	Grease leather and lay on gold leaf
N	R	L	Letter titles in gold or foil or transfer
N	R	L	Clean off surplus gold

A plough in use.

Kay Evans is sewing a book for the first time.

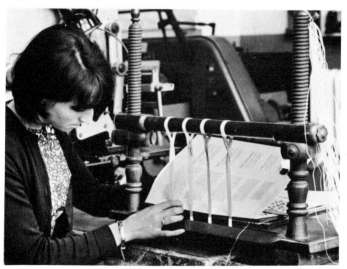

Simple inlaid and overlaid decoration.

A free adaptation of the front cover of a book on Mondrian, and two others that stemmed from it. These were done with transfer foil and letters.

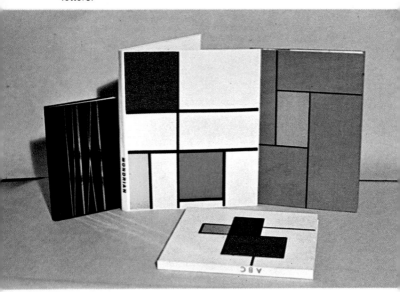

5 The first stage

The first bindings you do should be of plain paper, to give you the opportunity to carry out all the processes at an early stage: if you bind three of them, there will be a chance to correct any weaknesses that may be evident. You will need a bench, a bone folder, a nipping-press and pressing boards, a lying-press, spring dividers and a saw. Don't be terrified by this list - in the chapter on special equipment, there are suggested subsitutes. The materials will be 50 sheets of paper, 100 gsm, in one of the sizes known as demy, medium, royal, or A2; some ribbed kraft wrapping paper, 100 gsm; strawboard or millboard about the same thickness as eight leaves of this book; linen thread (35-2 cord), a needle, and some drawing pins or thumb tacks. Try to get paper with the grain in the short direction of the sheet.

Folding the sheets to make sections

Lay the sheets on the bench with a long edge near you; lift the near, right-hand corner of the top sheet and lay it on the left-hand corner; then, with the edge of a bone folder, set the fold. This makes a folio or 4-page section.

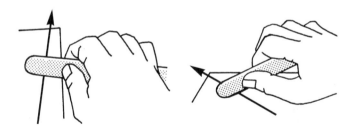

Now turn over the far end of the fold to the near end and set that to make a quarto or 8-page section. The last fold is made by bending the previous one from right to left to make an octavo or 16-page section. The crease that appears inside can be avoided by slitting the second fold a little more than half its length before making the last one. Try to avoid moving the near left-hand corner when folding - you will find it easier and more efficient. When all the sections are folded, knock them up level on the head (the folded top edge) and spine, and put them between boards in press. Be sure that none of the folds are overlapping, and press them overnight.

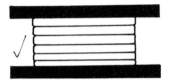 

Sewing

Holding the sections together by sewing the folded edges is the true binding of a book.

Before starting to sew, the positions for stitches must be marked on the sections. Cut some boards a little larger than the books; count off 16 sections, knock them up level on the head and spine between two boards, and put them in a lying press with the spine standing out about two inches (5 cms).

Use spring dividers and a pencil to mark the length of the book into five equal parts (A) so that you have four marks across the sections; then mark the width of the tape to the head from each of these marks (B). These eight marks show the tape positions; the other two marks (C) are shallow saw-cuts about half an inch (12 mm) from head and tail, and should not be visible in the middle of the sections. Make up three books of sixteen sections each.

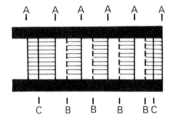

A sewing-frame will not be necessary if you use stiffened tape, but use one if you have it. You will need four tapes pinned around the rubber bands on the crossbar, with the book laid so that the marks on the spine can be used to locate the tapes, and the tapes held under the base by sewing keys or drawing pins. Place the sewing-frame so that the tapes are near the edge of the bench, and sit sideways so that your left arm can reach around the end of the frame. If you decide not to use a sewing-frame, four-inch (10 cm) lengths of tape, held to the edge of a softwood board by drawing pins, will stand up sufficiently to allow you to sew over them. The board should be larger than the book.

Treat the sections as if they had been printed, and put them on the bench where your left hand can reach them, with their backs away from the sewing position and the first one on top. Each section will be turned over, like the pages of a book, to put the fold against the tapes, and this ensures a correct sequence. You can number them if you wish - just to make sure.

Choose an appropriate thread. A thin thread for books with thin, numerous sections or hard paper; a thick one for thick sections or soft paper. Sewing will make the spine of a book thicker, and this can be useful: or a nuisance if it is overdone. A 'swell' of 25% is about right, but there is no rule. Winding thread around a pencil as many times as there are sections will give an idea of its bulk, but some will sink into the paper.

Turn the first section over to the tapes and open it to the centre. Keep your left hand inside, with the thumb and index finger in the angle of the fold; using the needle with your other hand, pierce the sewing marks - not your thumb. Then, with a thread five feet long, start sewing with single thread - in at the saw-cut, out and over the tape, in again, out and over the second tape, and so on to the other saw-cut.

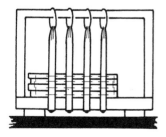 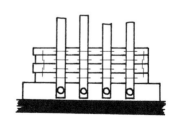

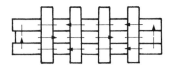

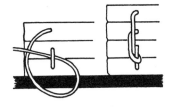

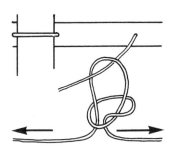

Use both hands to make sewing less laborious - it can be done. When the first section is sewn, pull the thread tight in the direction of the sewing (pulling at right angles may tear the paper) until three or four inches are left at the other end; then turn over the next section, put the needle through the saw-cut above the one from which it has come, and sew in the same way. Pull tight and double knot the two ends. Sew the third section and pull tight, then make a kettle stitch at the saw-cut by passing the needle and thread behind the thread joining the previous two sections and through the loop so formed; bring over the fourth section and carry on, treating them all like the third. Kettle stitches will form a chain of knots to hold the ends of sections together, and the last one is finished with two kettle stitches.

When the end of a thread is reached, a weaver's knot is used to tie on a new length. The stiffness of the thread must be reduced or it may slip, so be sure it is fast before cutting short the ends.

Looking inside the sections as you sew is cheating, but it does help when you are a beginner.

Endpapers

These are protective sheets at the ends of books: they are part of the binding, not of the book. You will need strong paper, slightly larger than an open section, with the grain in the short direction. Use the ribbed kraft paper for these books.

Tipped endpapers are the simplest. Fold two sheets in half, tip the folded edges with paste less than ¼" (6 mm) wide, and stick them to the first and last leaves of the book so that they are level with the spine and head.

Tipping is done by laying the sheet to be tipped on some waste paper, covering all but the edge to be pasted with a piece of waste, and applying paste - with a finger.

'Guarded' endpapers are similar, except that instead of being tipped on, they are joined to the end sections with fine stiffened cambric before sewing. These strips are called guards.

Cut two strips of cambric 1" (25 mm) in width and as long as the book. Paste them and lay the folds of the endpapers down so that only ¼" (6 mm) of the fabric shows; the fold of an end section goes on the rest, with the first or last page of the book up, leaving a gap equal to the thickness of a section. After a few minutes, turn the endpaper over the section. The cloth forms a hinge, and the sewing will hold everything. This is very strong.

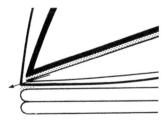

'Made' endpapers, with half the coloured sheet lined with white paper, are popular with binders who object to an opening that is not all one colour.

Lay a folded sheet of white paper on some waste paper, paste it, lay a folded coloured sheet on it - folded edge to folded edge - and press in clean boards for a few minutes before hanging up to dry. This makes an odd kind of three-leaf fold which may be guarded to the end section with cambric; alternatively, the white part of it can be tipped inside another folded white sheet and sewn on as a section. The sewing goes through the two white papers so that there are two leaves to the book and three away. After sewing, the back fold of a 'made and sewn' endpaper must be tipped to the section. The folded edges of endpapers must not be damaged, so the saw-cuts in the spine must be made before they are attached.

With three books on the go, you will have the opportunity to try out all these endpapers - but sorrow will be your lot if you haven't got the grain parallel to the spine of all those bits of paper. Cockling across the leaves will mean that you have gone wrong.

6   The second stage

Now that the books are firmly held by the sewing, the first requirement is satisfied. Some additional support will be needed to prevent loosening of the sections; the rough edges will collect dust, so you will need to cut them; and the shape of the spine must be fixed so that the books open and close well. You will need glue and a gluebrush, a plough, a hammer, backing boards, pressing tins, and mull.

Gluing-up

Gluing the back to stop the sections from moving is the first step. The glue should be hot (about 130° F; 55° C) and thin. Lay a piece of waste on the bench so that it hangs over the edge (A). Hold a book between the finger-tips of both hands and tap the folded edges - the spine and head - on the bench until all the sections are level and square. Lay the book down with the spine just beyond the edge of the bench and the tapes (B) kept out of the way with two pieces of millboard. Glue the spine with a stippling action to push the glue into the sections, then rub it in with your thumb. Before the glue sets, knock up the edges again and put the book aside. It is most important to have the edges level and square as the glue sets.

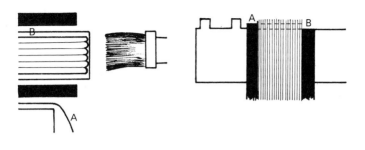

Edge-cutting

The edges of books are usually cut with a guillotine but, as it weighs over a ton, the traditional plough and lying-press will be better for you: many binders claim that the plough does a better job anyway. However, if you have access to a guillotine, use it - but be wary of the edge with chips that savages a book as if with fangs. Any edge for book-cutting must be perfect.

When the glue is set, lay the book on the bench and mark each side with lines, parallel to the spine, to show where the fore-edge is to be cut; a second line, farther from the spine, will be useful as a guide when putting the book in press. Aim to remove as little paper as possible - you can always cut off more. Have the lying-press turned over, with the plough guides on top and to your left, and open to about the thickness of the book.

Put a piece of millboard on each side of the book, laying one to the guide line A, the other to the cutting line B. Holding the book and boards firmly with one hand, lower them into the press and tighten enough to stop them from falling through. The guide line should be above the surface of the left cheek, the cutting line level with the right-hand one; look underneath to see that the spine is still square and not twisted in any way, then tighten the screws. Be sure that the gaps at each end of the press are equal - it indicates that pressure is even all along the book. The fore-edge is now ready for cutting.

Now check the plough-knife - the underside must be quite flat and the edge of the knife must be very sharp.

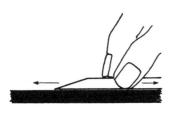

A blunt edge makes hard work and tears the paper.
When grinding is necessary and the flat surface needs honing, turn to the narrow surface of the oil-stone, as it gets little use and is probably flat; lay the knife flat on that and don't hold it - just move the knife with your fingertips. The slightest bevel on the underside will cause the knife to rise as it cuts.

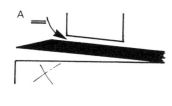

The plough, with a knife in it, must be tested by running it on the press to be sure that the knife clears the surface. If it is high, pack one or two thicknesses of paper between the blade and the inside plate (A): if low, pack under the outer plate (B). Too much packing makes the knife lower than the plough edge, and the right-hand cheek will rock on it.

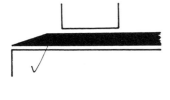

Now start cutting. The knife must be clear of the book at first, but as you move the plough to and fro and tighten the screw very slightly each time at your end, it will start to cut. The more you cut with one stroke, the nearer you'll be to disaster - if the offcuts crinkle, it's a warning that the screw has been turned too much or the knife is blunt.

Always remove any paper from under the knife, or it will rise and the book will be cut in steps instead of being smooth.

When all the paper is cut,
take the book from the press
and use a strip of waste paper
to check if the sides are parallel
by measuring the width
at head and tail.

Cut the tail next. Bend the
outside leaf over so that
the newly cut edge is exactly
over the line of the spine,
and mark through the edge with
a knife to show where the cut
is to be - this gives two marks
at right-angles to the parallel
edges. Putting the book in press
is slightly complicated by the
swell of the sewing, but you can
overcome that by standing the
book on its head and interleaving
with waste paper until the
thickness is the same
from spine to fore-edge.

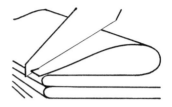

When cutting the tail and the head, the back folds of the
sections must be toward you, and it is important to cut only
on the forward stroke to avoid tearing the backs of the
sections.

Presses and ploughs are not to be had in every toolshop,
so you may have to use some form of cutting clamp. If you
do, remember that a sharp knife is needed, that it should be
ground on one side only, and that it must be held at a right-
angle to the book.

In all cutting it is essential that the book is not twisted in
any way.

The spine

A proper development of the spine (which is often called
the back) is the most important contribution to the good
appearance, effective opening and closing, and long life of
a book. It can overcome, to some extent, paper that has the
grain in the wrong direction or is too stiff, but it will not
prevent physical deterioration.

Your choice of sewing thread should have made the spine thicker than the rest of the book, and this swelling will help to round and back it with a minimum of force. Rounding curves the spine; and backing produces the grooves in which the boards fit and makes the spine more rigid vertically, while the slight bending of the paper in the joint allows a better opening of the book. The diagrams show that the line of the backs of the sections becomes curved, but remains virtually the same length from shoulder to shoulder.

Before starting this work, the glue must be softened or it may break the paper. Paste does this well (it is 90% water and stays where you put it), so rub some on the glue and leave the book until it is no longer tacky.

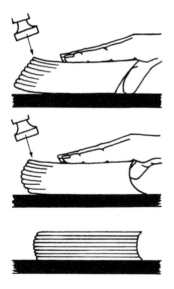

Rounding

This is done with a hammer and you need not fear for the book: paper is re-arranged wood fibre and is stronger than most timbers. Lay the book on a solid surface with its spine away from you; fan out the leaves so that the upper part is pulled to you and, with the book flat, hammer along the shoulder. This knocks the whole book sideways, but turning it over and repeating the action will make it round. Keep on doing this until the book has a semi-elliptic shape. The degree of roundness depends upon the book and your personal likes and dislikes.

Backing

The turning over of the backs
of the sections is almost
automatic if a little swell
remains after rounding. Put a
backing board under the tapes
on each side of the book,
with a space between its sharp
edge and the fold of the endpaper
that is equal to the thickness
of board that will be used
for the cover - never less.
Have the lying-press open and
lower into it the book and boards;
if you have judged the opening
well, they will wedge and you
need only adjust it so that no
more than the thickness of
the board projects above
the press. Before tightening,
be sure that there is a similar
amount of book standing out
of the press on both sides and
that the edges are level.
As you tighten the press, the
book will be squeezed under
the swell and your hammering
will turn the sections down
to the backing boards. The glue
must be soft before you do
any hammering.

Hold the hammer lightly
just below the head and,
with its face down, practice a
sideways flick with your wrist
to get the proper action. It
is very important to avoid direct
blows which cause sections
to collapse instead of turning
over, so every stroke must be a
glancing one away from
the centre of the spine.

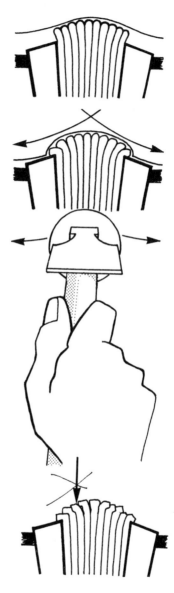

Pick on a section about four from the centre and, using it as a target, tap gently along its length; then deal with its opposite number in the same way. You will see that the edge of the spine has gone closer to the backing board. Now do the same to the sections about three from the sides, then go back to the centre again. Do this until you can see that the sections are evenly turned down at each end and the lines along the spine are parallel. Kinks in the lines of sections are usually caused by direct blows - they are difficult to put right.

Cleaning off

This is rarely done nowadays, but it makes a book so much better that it is worth while. In spite of the fact that the glue has been kept flexible during working, the paper under it has been nearly dry and the back will tend to flatten as the book is used. To ensure that it does keep its shape, take the book from the press after backing, lay pressing tins into the joint under the tapes, and put the book back into press between pressing boards with the tapes inside. The correct shape of the book at this stage is most important, because it will be fixed like that when you've finished. Lay a generous coat of paste on the spine and leave it to soak in for fifteen minutes. Then, with the end of a wooden ruler held at an angle of 45°, scrape the spine clean. Paste again, lightly, and rub it clean with screwed up paper or edge trimmings. The water from the paste soaks into the paper fibres and softens them; the scraping, done with some force, removes the paste and any glue that is not between the sections, and moulds the wet paper into shape; the final rub-down smooths the surface. You must leave the book in press until next day to let it dry. When this is done, the shape will be permanent, so be sure it is right before you start.

First and second linings

Mull, a stiffened crash material, and brown paper linings give added strength and protection to the spine. The grain of the paper must be along the spine.

Put the fore-edge of the book in the lying-press, glue the spine slightly, and lay on a piece of mull cut so that it will be ¼" (6 mm) short of the head and tail and have a 1"

(25 mm) flap at each side. Avoid getting glue on the tapes and mull that are not on the spine, and always brush clear of the head and tail. If you get glue on the edge of a book, let it dry - it will come off more easily then. You will only push it into the fibre while it is wet.

Glue the spine again and cover it with brown paper; damp the surface to soften the fibres and rub down thoroughly with the edge of a bone folder. When it is dry, the long edges can be folded back and slit to remove the paper that is not on the spine; trim the ends with shears. Always let linings dry well before continuing work, and put the book down on a board thick enough to keep it from resting on the shoulder.

Hollow backs

Hollow back lining is a stronger form of paper lining - usually associated with leather bindings, but sometimes with cloth. Glue the spine lightly and, using a piece of paper four times the spine width, lay one edge to the left side; fold exactly to the other side (1) and peel it off. Use the edge of the narrow flap as the gauge for a second fold; glue the flap and put the larger one down on it (2) to make a flat tube exactly the width of the spine. Glue the spine well, but thinly, and lay the single thickness of the tube on it; rub down well, fold back the surplus paper, and trim off (3). An extra thickness of paper is often added to make a firmer hollow. Cut the ends level at head and tail.

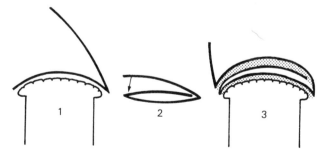

7 The third stage

The lining of the spine completes the structural work on a book; all that is needed to complete protection is a hard cover with hinges to allow it to open. Covers made off the book are called 'cases' - they consist of two boards and a central lining strip, covered with cloth, paper, leather, or any combination of these.

Board cutting

The board used for covers is usually 20″ x 25″ (50 cm x 65 cm) or larger, so cut it down to a little over the size that you need. Rough cutting can be done by scoring each side with a knife and bending the board to break it. The grain must be parallel to the spine. Use the plough and press, or a cutting clamp and knife, to cut boards accurately to fit each book. After the first long edge is cut, use a carpenter's square and a knife to mark accurate cutting positions. Cut boards with a projection at head and tail of one tenth of an inch (2½ mm), and cut the fore-edge level with the end-papers when the back edge is in the joint. When the cover is made, there will be a groove in the joint and the case will stand out to protect the edge of the book. The central strip can be cut from manilla card - it should be the width of the spine and the length of the boards.

Case-making

Cut bookcloth 1″ (25 mm) wider than the length of boards and 2″ (50 mm) longer than the distance from fore-edge to fore-edge around the spine of the book. All paper, boards, and cloth should have grain parallel to the spine.

You will need thin, hot glue or PVA cold adhesive, a glue brush, scissors, a bone folder, and waste paper to glue on. When using hot glue, speed is important, so arrange the bench to have a working space, a place for gluing out, and the glue-pot, in that order from left to right - or the other way round if you are left-handed.

Stand the book on end with its boards projecting ⅛" (3 mm) at the fore-edge, and measure the distance between the back edges of the boards (AB) with a strip of paper.

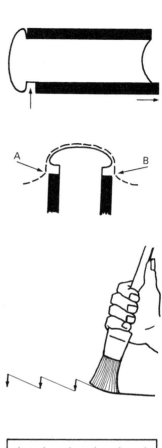

On the reverse side of the cloth, draw a line ½" (12 mm) from one long edge; lay a board to the line with its edge ½" from the end of the cloth, and draw a line along the other edge; from this last line, mark the width between the boards in two places and draw lines through the marks. If you use the lines as a guide, the covers will fit when they are made. Gluing is done with a stippling movement of the brush to spread glue without leaving brush marks. Some practice on waste paper will help to give the feel of the brush. Lay the cloth on waste paper twice its size; take the brush from the glue and scrape out the surplus on the crossbar until it will not drip, then use a wrist action to apply the glue. As you can see in the drawing, the bristles are pointing slightly forward; the action produces a series of dabs which, if the brush gets pressed hard enough, will join and cover the surface. Follow a pattern to avoid missing out any of the cloth. Hold the point 1 and work away from it; then move to 2, 3 and so on.

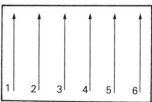

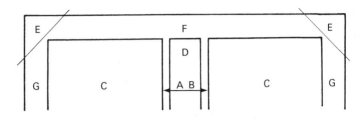

When that is finished, you may need to touch in the parts where your finger was. Put the brush back on the crossbar, and start covering.

Lay the boards (C) to the centre guide lines, with the strip of manilla (D) between them. Move the cloth from the waste paper to your working position, trim the long end to ½″ width, and cut the corners (E) at an angle of 45° with the cut a little more than the thickness of the board away from the corner of the board. Now turn in the long edges (F), tuck in the four corners, and turn in the short edges (G). Rub down the cloth all over with a bone folder.

Put the book in its case so that the 'squares' are the same all round, and press in the groove with the edge of a folder - but do be careful not to split the groove.

Before completing this part of the work by 'casing-in' (fixing the book in its case), you can do any lettering or decoration that you have planned. If you don't care for the result, it is then possible to make a new case without undoing any work.

Casing-in

When the case is finished, one endpaper can be pasted, with special attention to the mull and tapes in the joint. Paste along the joint with a stippling action, then hold the book steady, with a finger on the centre tape, and brush away from that point. Be sure to clear the edge with every stroke - stopping on the edge will double the paper on itself with dreadful results. Then close the book and, if the squares are not even, slide it into position. Do not open the board.

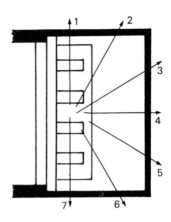

Paste down the other endpaper in the same way, close the board, adjust the squares if necessary, and give the book a light nip between pressing boards laid to the grooves for about ten minutes. Only then should you open the book: but if the temptation to do so overcomes you before it has been pressed, the endpaper will probably slide along the board and a crease will form along the edge of the mull. By the way, if you did get paste inside the endpapers all is not lost. Slip a piece of waxed paper in, give the book a nip, take it out and wash the paste off with moist cotton wool. Put in another sheet of waxed paper and leave it there until the endpaper has dried.

A stronger method for putting down endpapers is to glue the paper, with the tapes and mull held clear, put in a manilla card to fit into the joint but ⅜" (10 mm) short of the three edges, then glue that and the tapes and mull in the normal way. This makes a very strong joint, especially if linen tape has been used. If paste is used, the boards will warp too much.

When the endpapers are dry enough to take full pressure, put brass rods or knitting needles in the grooves and press the book with the edges of the pressing boards on the rods. Press overnight or longer.

Case-making so far has dealt with traditional materials which are no more interesting than those chosen by most publishers. You need not be so limited in your choice, and if you see a fabric that you think would look well on a book, you can experiment. All that is necessary is to prevent glue from passing through the hessian, burlap, brocade, printed cotton, or linen that you fancy: a lining of paper will do that.

Cut two pieces of thin bank paper (30 to 45 gsm) a little larger than the cloth. Cover them evenly with thin PVA adhesive, put them face to face and strip them apart immediately to even out brush marks. When the surface is tacky, lay the fabric on one of the sheets and smooth it down gently with your hand. If there are no creases, the other sheet can be discarded. Very light pressing is permitted, but too much will force the PVA through the cloth. When this is dry, use it in the same way as bookcloth except at the corners, where the absence of filling will cause fraying if a cut is made. Universal corners do not fray - you make them by turning in the corners, instead of cutting them off, before turning in the edges of the cloth.

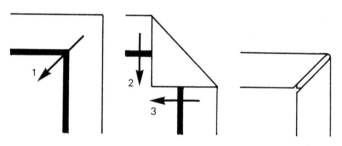

This corner wears well but is clumsy with thick fabrics. It has been very popular for reference books in public libraries and, even if the corners of the boards collapse because of rough treatment, there is no cut edge to open and fray. Rounded corners last even better, but not many books look well with round-cornered pages, so it will be necessary to keep the rounding of the board to a minimum if you still want square pages. In larger books, for which heavier cloth is suitable, the squares can be larger, and a slightly rounded corner will not be out of place. The corners of the boards need rounding before a start is made on covering. Before turning in the edges of the cloth, cut the corners about ⅜" from the board, turn in the edges and pleat in the fabric, using a folder or an awl. A hammer may also be useful if it is used discreetly.

Any paper, even if it is not intended for making book-covers, may be used if it is protected. There are many self-adhesive transparent plastic films available, and some of them have a matt surface if you dislike glossy covers. Melinex film is very suitable for this form of protection. It will be better to line the paper with film before making the case as a rule; but if it is to be decorated after covering, the film goes on later.

Try to avoid glue marks on your cases; if you do get them, they should be left to dry until scratching with a finger nail makes them turn pale, and then removed with a piece of Cellotape, Scotch tape, or a damp finger. PVA adhesive can, sometimes, be removed with an eraser after it has set. These methods will only work on smooth bookcloth: paper and fibrous surfaces just have to be kept clean.

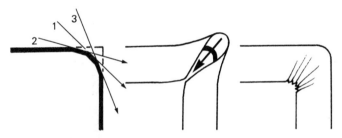

Finishing

The title of a book is lettered across, up, or down the spine in gold or colour. The first is the most usual; the second was peculiar to Britain, and the last is now generally used.

The impressing of letters and decoration in bookbinding is called 'finishing'. The letters are engraved on the ends of brass tools set in wooden handles; only capital letters are used, and a set of forty tools includes the numerals and stops. These, in skilled hands, produce the best results on individual work.

The cost of brass hand-letters is high, so many binders use a type-holder in which a line of type can be set. Brass type is needed for continuous work, but you will find that Monotype, or the stronger founders' type, will serve very well if you don't overheat it. These are individual pieces of type that can be used again and again: and, if you do melt them, the cost is low. The type-holder is a box about 4" x ¾" (100 mm x 20 mm), with one long side adjustable to hold the line straight, and a screw at one end to keep the type from moving. The base of the box is on a tang that fits into a wooden handle, and the long fixed edge is bevelled to allow you to see the top edge of the type. A great advantage of using printers' type is that the range of sizes and typefaces is almost infinite - and slightly worn type gives much brighter impressions than new.

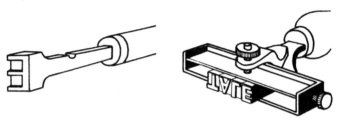

The gold or colour for this work is bought in the form of blocking foil - a thin plastic ribbon, in various widths, with a minute deposit of gold on one side and a coating of heat-sensitive adhesive on the gold. Some of the coloured foils have an adhesive included in the pigment. Real gold is obtainable, but there are many substitutes - very much cheaper - that do as well. The adhesive side of the foil is laid on the cloth, a hot tool is applied, and the gold sticks in the impression.

Set the first line of a title to go across the spine of a book so that you can look down the bevel at the top edge of the type. Use an ink pad to make a proof copy for correct spelling and spacing, and make corrections if necessary. The spacing of letters is the apparent area between them: this should be uniform throughout the line, so decide which pair of letters is most widely spaced and open up the rest to match. It's easier to see irregularities if the proof is turned

A type-holder and hand letters on the finishing-stove. (The pieces of type are only there to show their appearance.)

Dave Collins lettering the spine of a book with hand letters and gold foil.

upside-down so that the word is not being read so easily. Clean the type with a small brush and benzene to remove the colour. Dirty type makes dirty work.

Cut a piece of foil wider than the spine, and use a needle to draw very fine lines to indicate the top edge of each line of lettering. Scotch tape the ends to the sides of the book, and mark the centre of the spine over each line.

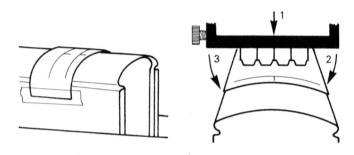

Heat the typeholder until it just hisses when touched with a licked finger. Then, with the book in a lying-press so that you can get over the spine, put the centre of the line of type under the centre mark on the foil, with the guide line still visible. Rock the typeholder to the left and right and lift it. The whole contact must be very quick and nearly in one movement.

When the foil is removed, the impressions should have clear outlines. If the gold does not stick, the tool was not hot enough or the impression not sufficiently firm: if the insides of the letters are blocked up and the edges ragged, the tool was too hot or contact too long. If rubbing with a woollen rag does not remove the surplus, try lifting it off with Scotch tape quickly applied and taken off. If you need to go over the impressions again, put the type in some letters that are right, slip an edge of foil into position, and bring the tool across over the foil.

Lettering along the spine is not so simple with a type-holder, because the whole line comes into contact at the same time: but if you can make, or have made, a type clamp - to hold single types - the letters can be struck individually.

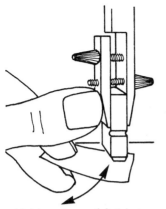

Make a pattern of the impressions at the edge of a piece of paper, put it in position on the book and Scotch tape along the top of the lettering. Fold back the paper with the Scotch tape as a hinge. If the letters are put in under the paper pattern, they will be correctly placed. Arrange the type that you need on the bench and put the clamp to get hot, with the first letter in it.

Hold a piece of foil between the index and middle fingers of your left hand, in such a way that with the hot tool poised over the place where the impression is to be, it can be steadied with the left thumb, the foil slipped under, and the impression made. It all reads like a conjuring trick, but is fairly simple in fact. Once the type-clamp is hot, the heating of the next piece of type will not take long and you'll soon learn to handle it without really touching hot metal. This method can be used on the sides of books; and it is good practice for the time when you become the proud owner of traditional hand-letters.

The development of Letraset and other transfer sheets puts good lettering within the powers of people who have no special training in the art. Many good type-faces are available, and it is only necessary to put the letter in position and rub to transfer it to any smooth surface. If the position is wrong, Scotch tape removes it: if right, a spray of cellulose lacquer will make it permanent. The white letters have the widest application for your work.

Make every effort to get lettering right - it is such an obvious feature that everybody notices it; bad lettering can spoil the appearance of a binding which, in every other respect, may be excellent.

8 Rebinding a book

Now that you know how books are bound, the time has come to rebind one that is falling apart. Choose one that isn't in very bad condition to start with, and check it through to see that all the pages and illustrations are complete. This is called collating and should be done before pulling any book to pieces.

Pulling

The process of separating the sections is made easier if the glue on the spine is broken away from the paper. Hold the book in your left hand and bang the spine on a bench to flatten it; grip the book so that it remains square, lay it on its side, and tap along the joint with a hammer. This flattens the joint a little, and may jump the linings off the spine; if it does, the glue will go with them and the sections will separate easily: if not, more force will be needed. Open the book to the first page - the endpaper on one side and the half-title on the other is the usual form - close the book with your thumbs inside, grip firmly, and open it again. This should pull the endpaper away from the first page: if it doesn't, try again.

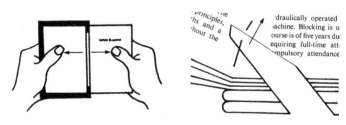

Most books have sections of sixteen pages, so count the first four leaves (8 pages) and look to see if the thread is there. Cut it before turning the next four leaves to the end of the section. If the book has been made on formal lines, you should find a letter B or number 2 on page 17. These 'signatures' are to mark the first page of each section, and will guide you when pulling. Sections may have 8, 12, 16, 24, or 32 pages, but 16 and 32 are the most common. When you have found the beginning of the second section, put your thumbs in once more, grip with the book closed, and open again to make the sections separate. If the threads are all cut, the first section may come clean away, but it will probably need a little coaxing. Carry on until all the sections are separated, and use the signatures as a guide all the time. It is an interesting reflection on printers that they usually use the Latin alphabet for signatures - no J, V, or W.

A word of warning here. If there are illustrations on a paper differing from the rest of the book, they will not, usually, be numbered with the pages, and they may be wrapped around the sections (they are in this book): if they are wrapped around, include them in the sections when you are pulling.

You may find, after starting to pull a book, that there are no sections - that the leaves are all separate. This is unsewn binding, not a new problem, and it is dealt with in another chapter.

As you pull the book, use a knife to remove any glue from the backs of the sections, and take out all the ends of thread. As the glue comes away, it will take with it some paper fibre. If you hold an outside leaf to the light, the thinned portion will be more translucent than the rest. This will be made good later.

Pressing

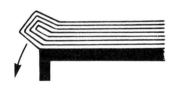

Before putting the sections in press, the bent-up backs should be straightened by laying them, one by one, on the edge of a pressing board and bending them down with the palm of the hand. This makes it easier to put them in press, where they should stay all night.

Guarding

This strengthens the thinned or torn backs of sections, joins loose leaves, and gives a new surface for the glue to hold.

Guards are narrow strips of thin, preferably rag, paper: best quality bank paper of 45 gsm for most books; but if the paper of the book is thin, a guarding paper of 30 gsm will be needed. Using thick paper to mend a thin one is not a good idea. These papers are usually obtainable in the size 21″ x 16½″, or in the continental A2 which is a little longer. Fold it in four and cut strips about ⅜″ wide (10 mm), with the grain along the strips - have them a little longer than the sections, and remember that few sections need more than one guard.

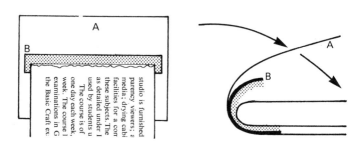

Lay an even coating of paste on a sheet of glass; tear the folded end from four guards and lay them side by side on the paste. If they crinkle across the width, throw them out - they're the wrong way of the grain and you will have to cut new ones. Peel up a guard (B) and lay it, paste side up, on a sheet of thin waste paper (A); put the first section on it so that the back of the section covers half the width of the guard, and draw the waste sheet over to stick the other half of the guard to the section. Dust with French chalk (talc powder) and lay the section to one side. Do this to all the sections, then leave them under a weight to dry before pressing. If a book has loose plates, or even some that are still tipped in, they can be firmly attached with guards before doing the backs of the sections.

When the sections are taken from the press, cut off the ends of the guards, examine them to be sure that they are still in correct order, and mark the spine for sewing. If the endpapers were made while the book was being pressed, you can go right ahead with the sewing.

Repairing torn paper

There are occasions when you may want to mend leaves, and the repairs can be almost invisible. The paste for this work is made from one part of corn starch in ten parts of water (by weight). Mix the starch in a little water to a smooth paste, stir in the rest of the water and boil it gently for 10 to 15 minutes. Keep it stirred while it cools, to break down gel formation. This paste is almost clear when it dries.

Look at a tear in a printed sheet and you will see that the edges overlap. They must go back as they were when you join them. Lay a piece of long-fibred white tissue under the leaf, with its grain across the tear. The best paper for this is Japanese; it has long fibres and is very thin. Starting at the end of the tear, use a watercolour brush to paste the edges and join them. You may find that the overlap changes sides, so be careful to follow the change. As you work along, lay another piece of tissue over the wet paste: it will stick, but there should be so little paste that you will be able to pull away the tissue when it is dry, leaving only a few fibres to reinforce the repair. If the tissue tears, a rubber eraser will remove any excess.

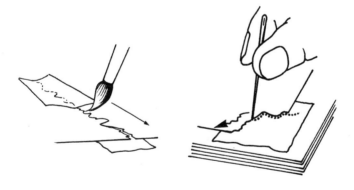

Torn-off corners can be filled in with paper similar to the rest of the sheet - repairers never throw out old paper - but a similarity of thickness and texture is more important than colour. Put the new paper on a pad of blotting paper, lay the damaged sheet over it and prick the outline of the tear in the new paper. Make the holes very close together and tear along the line of the perforations. The torn edges can be pasted to each other, using the same method as before, and any surplus paper cut off to make the edges straight.

Another problem is the leaf with frail edges. This is common in music scores where the title page, oddly enough, seems to suffer a lot of hardship. The best method of dealing with it is to reinforce the whole leaf. Never patch paper - if the patch shrinks more than the leaf, a pucker will form along its edge. You will have to line both sides: a lining on one side causes the leaf to curl as the lining paper shrinks. The thin Japanese tissue is best for this, though acid-free tissue of the type used by jewellers will serve.

Cut two pieces of tissue large enough to project all round the leaf. Use ordinary paste, thinned with water until it is sloppy, to paste a sheet of glass; lay the leaf to be strengthened on the paste, and paste over it. Lay one piece of tissue over the leaf and paste that. Now, very carefully, lift the whole lot from the glass and turn it over to carry out the same procedure on the other side. Lay it between two sheets of clean blotting paper and leave it to dry before putting it in press. Whole books can be done this way! Some loss of clarity is inevitable, but the book is preserved. There has been some research into this subject by W. H Langwell, with particular reference to the preservation of records, and his POSTLIP laminating materials are easily available with instructions for their use.

Most repair work should be done before guarding the sections, and it may even be necessary to split a sheet at the back fold and guard the halves together after the work is done. Simple tears can be repaired, even if the book has been bound, if they are not too near the spine.

Always be aware of the grain of paper made after 1800 - it may have been made by machine. The rule that grain should be from head to tail is not observed by printers, and you must copy the grain direction with your repair materials. The only exception is in the mending of tears: the few fibres that remain will not shrink strongly enough to pull the page. Guarding sections is a different affair - it must always be done with the grain along the fold. Try it the wrong way once - just to see what happens.

9 Unsewn binding

Books made from single leaves are the price we pay for cheap books, but the early form - the 'perfect' binding - was intended to deal with the problem of joining the sheets of books with coloured illustrations that would stick if laid face to face: they were not cheap. Caoutchouc (raw rubber) was the adhesive, and it seemed that a new era in bookbinding had arrived. But it didn't last, and that was less than a century ago

Modern adhesives may be more successful. Polyvinyl acetate (PVA) emulsion adhesives rely for success on the paper fibre being long enough to hold the weight of the leaf, and on being able to survive flexing and tension as the book is used: others appear to hold the spine so rigid that there is no flexing.

In commercial production, sheets are folded and gathered into order; the back edges are sawn or ground off, glued, and a cover is applied to the glue. When the edges have been cut, the book is ready to use. A recent development leaves the folded ends of the sections - only the central part is ground away. It is very efficient and looks like a sewn book. This is difficult to recognise.

Unsewn books in need of binding have usually fallen apart, so check the pages and illustrations for correct order and completeness, and straighten any turned-down corners; earlier treatment saves a lot of work. The spine will have become concave so hammer it, as in rounding, until it is straight; remove the cover, and cut two boards a little larger than you will need for the new binding. If the book had tipped-on endpapers, half has been left on each end leaf and these should be removed.

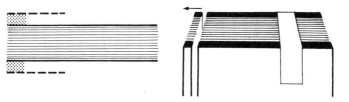

Cut two pieces of stiffened cambric 1½" (35 mm) in width and the length of the book. Tip them on instead of end-papers, and put the book between the pieces of millboard. The width of paste when tipping should be ¼", because part of it will be cut away. Knock up the fore-edge and the boards to make them flush and square, and Scotch tape the head and tail tightly to hold the book together. Cut the fore-edge if it is dirty, then cut off the spine to remove the adhesive. You now have a bundle of leaves held together by Scotch tape. Put the book in a lying-press with 4" (10 cm) standing out; roughen the whole surface with a saw and make cuts as shown to a depth of one tenth of an inch (2½ mm).

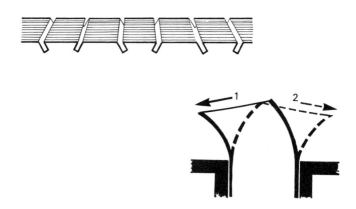

Brush on PVA and bend the book from side to side as you rub in the adhesive, then clean out the sawcuts. As soon as the PVA has set, remove the book from the press and take off the boards; hold it very firmly and round the spine slightly. Put the book back in press, lay nylon threads in the cuts, rub in PVA to hold them there, cut off the ends to ¼" and stick them to the cambric parallel to the spine. Take out of the press again to fold back the cambric, tip on endpapers over it so that they are level with the back edge of the end leaf on each side, and glue the cambric down on the endpaper.

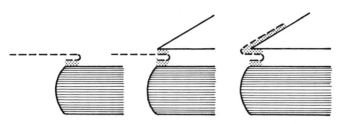

All that remains now is to cut the head and tail, if they need it, and trim the endpapers with a knife; back the book, and line it with mull and paper. Use PVA for this, as glue will not stick to PVA once it has set. The rest is case-making and finishing in the ordinary way.

This makes a good binding for text books, but some of the refinements are not needed for light paperbacks. For these, the cambric can be left out and an ordinary endpaper tipped on with PVA, after the sawcuts have been made and the ends of the nylon stuck down. Some rounding is necessary to counter the tendency to concave spines.

A very simple binding is useful for storing typescripts and loose-leaf notes that may be wanted some time.

Put the sheets between boards with Scotch tape to hold them at head and tail; cut off the spine, rough up the surface, and make sawcuts at 1″ intervals. Apply PVA, and let it dry with the spine square before taking it from the press. Remove the Scotch tape, and peel the boards from the book; if the end sheet comes away, tip it on with PVA. Tip on folded endpapers and another single sheet of waste paper outside them. Glue the boards and stick one on each waste sheet, with a good, unsawn edge ¼″ from the spine; nip them lightly. If the margins are good enough, you can cut the edges: if not, the boards should be flush on all three edges.

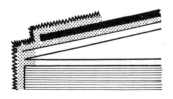

Put the book in the lying-press and give the spine a thin coat of PVA without bending it. Cut a piece of unbleached linen (any unfilled cloth will do) the length of the spine, and wide enough to cover the spine and 1″ of the boards. Apply PVA to a sheet of glass, lay the linen on it to pick up the adhesive and put it on the book.

Make sure that it sticks to the spine, joints and boards, and cut off the ends. Some binders cut the head and tail at this stage. The boards may be covered with paper or book-cloth, laid to overlap the linen by $\frac{1}{4}''$ and turned in as for case-making. Glue down the endpapers, press lightly, and leave under a weight to dry.

The two outer books were done with fillets and gold foil: the centre ones with transfer foil.

The paper cover of this book from Maidstone College of Art was used to decorate the binding.

Transfer letters being applied.

The red and the black books have been lettered by traditional means: the rest are transfer work.

Library bindings in quarter-leather with cloth or printed paper sides. They have been in use for 25 years or more.

A spokeshave being used to thin leather all over.

10 Sewing unsewn books

Unsewn bindings are useful, but they rarely open as well as sewn ones: if you have good books to bind, there are better ways of dealing with them. The leaves can be joined by thin paper guards in order to form sections, and the sewing and binding can follow the usual course.

Good rag paper of 30 gsm is needed for the guards; they should be narrow - preferably not over ⅜″ wide (10 mm) - and you will need one for every two leaves. This paper is about .00125″ thick (.03 mm) and, as there will be one piece on the back edge of each leaf, a swell will form in the spine before the book is sewn. A book of 200 pages has 100 leaves, so the added paper will be .00125″ x 100 or .125″ - say ⅛″ (.03 mm x 100 equals 3 mm).

Cut off the spine of the book to remove the adhesive and divide the book into sections according to the signatures, or by counting off eight leaves at a time.

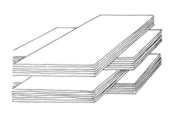

Stack the sections criss-cross to keep the leaves from becoming mixed. Take the first group of eight, open it to the centre, and lay it open on the bench. Paste the sheet of glass and lay four guards on the paste - and don't forget that crinkling across the guard means wrong grain direction, which can have devastating results in this type of work.

Use a thin sheet of waste paper to lay the guard on, paste side up, then take the two top leaves, put them face to face, lay the back edge to cover half the width of the guard, and draw over the waste to stick down the other half - just as already described when guarding orthodox sections. Dust with French (powdered) chalk, place the next two leaves in position before and after the guarded ones, and join them together: French chalk, two more leaves, and another guard - the next one completes the section. It isn't difficult, but it is a job that demands clean working and absolute control of the paste. All these pasted strips will take a fair time to dry, dependent on the atmosphere, so don't attempt to press them until you are sure that the paste will not be squeezed through to make a solid block of the back - it's a form of unsewn binding, but not one that you need. Before leaving the book in press, have it out to see that there is no sticking. Books made up in this manner must be sewn with very thin thread or the swelling will be too great.

Overcasting or oversewing

This method of making up sections is inferior to guarding, but has been much used to overcome the difficulty of dealing with books that have been bound so often that the backs of the sections are gone. Try it on some typescript with wide margins, for which it is very good, or a paperback that doesn't matter. You may find it useful.

Cut off the spine in the usual way, glue it with thin, hot glue, and leave it to dry. Separate the leaves to form groups of reasonable thickness, and oversew along the spines, using thin thread with a stitch every ½″ (B). The stitches should be less than ⅛″ from the edge, and you may find it helpful to make the holes with a needle held in a pin-vice (A).

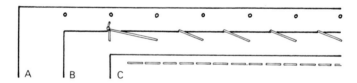

Another way is to stitch along the spine with a domestic sewing-machine that will do six or less stitches to an inch: if they are much nearer, they form a perforation (C).

Overcasting does not allow a book to open well into the spine, but it permits the use of tapes for sewing on, and the binding will be stronger, even though the sewing can never be as firm as on folded sheets. When sewing overcast sections, a sawcut for the kettle stitch is useless, so make the kettle stitch at a point beyond the knotted ends of the overcasting.

Side-sewing

This is a binding that is only suitable for thin paper with the grain along the spine, as there is no flexing of the back. The Chinese and Japanese use it for the thin, silky paper that is used for their best books.

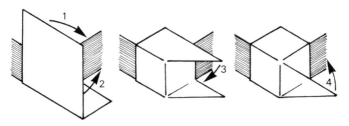

The oriental style is done by levelling the edges of the leaves, glueing a piece of coloured paper or cloth over the ends of the spine as shown, drilling or spiking three or five holes through the book, about $\frac{3}{8}''$ from the edge of the spine, and lacing a thread or cord through the holes. The covers are often of paper, covered with another printed paper which is turned in all round to fit the book exactly. These are sewn on at the same time as the sheets are sewn.

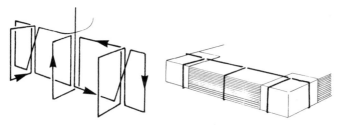

If you decide to use this form of binding and want stiff covers, they are simple to make but must be hinged to let the book open. Each board must be in two pieces, with a gap between them: the narrow strip, through which the sewing will go, is about $\frac{1}{2}''$ in width. If the turn-in at the spine is left wide enough, it can be used as an added strength in the hinge.

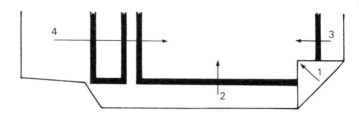

The western form of this is very strong and has a case-bound appearance. The spine is levelled or cut, and glued; endpapers are tipped on; a piece of cloth, cut on the cross to allow it to stretch when the book is backed, is glued to the spine and about 1½″ of each endpaper. A series of holes is drilled along the book - they can be about 1″ apart and ¼″ from the edge of the spine, and must go straight through while the book is held quite square. A hemp or nylon cord is used to saddle stitch the sheets, and if the stitching starts at the central hole, the ends need only be stuck down.

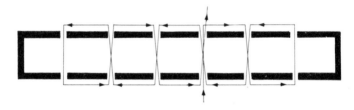

This kind of book can't be rounded, but the backs of the sheets can be turned over to form a joint and a slight curve, because the lining, being 'on the cross', will stretch. When the case is being made, provision must be made for a groove about ¼″ in width; the strip in the spine can be thicker than usual, as it will not need to bend when the book is opened. The outstanding example of this style of binding is the **Encyclopaedia Britannica**: it attracts no attention because the paper is made to suit it and the margins are wide enough to make it unnecessary to open right into the spine. This is really well designed.

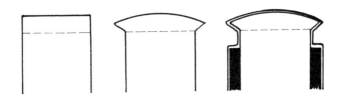

A useful form of photograph album can be made by using a variant of the oriental side-sewing method. It has the properties of a loose-leaf binding, as pages can be added or removed easily. The size of page that you use may be decided, to some extent, by the dimensions of sheets that are available: ignore the convention that the short side of an album is the binding edge - easy opening and correct grain direction are more important.

When you make a book with the intention of putting in more paper (photographs, news cuttings) after the binding

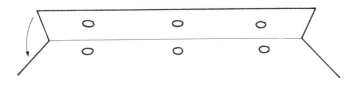

is complete, you must bind added thickness into the spine to prevent bulging. This can be done by doubling the thickness of the back edges of the leaves. Cut the paper to the leaf size of the book at head and tail, but make the fore-edge to back dimension ¾″ longer than you want it to finish. Use a millboard cut to leaf width as a gauge against which to bend over the extra ¾″ of each leaf, and use the same board, with three holes punched through it, to enable you to punch all the leaves accurately. The covers can be made as two separate boards, hinged ¾″ from the spine and punched to correspond with the leaves - and don't for-

get to make an allowance for the difference caused by the boards being larger than the book. Alternatively, you can make a case, using five pieces of board to give four hinges, which will look neater and be much firmer than the separate boards. There is no rule about the size to punch holes, but ¼″ holes at ½″ from the back edge will work very well.

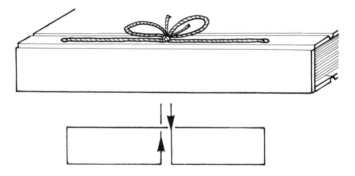

The inside of the case should be reinforced at the hinges with cloth cut shorter than the boards, and two of the album leaves will provide a lining for the insides. Lace through the holes with silk or leather thong, and the album will be complete and ready for use.

11 Library binding in leather

Books like dictionaries, that are in constant use, need very strong bindings that open easily and lie flat. In order to achieve this, they can be bound with leather-covered spines in such a way that the leather combines the functions of back-lining and cover.

In this form of binding, the spine must be made with great care; boards with a split back edge will be glued around the tapes before the cover is put on, and the leather will show small bumps across the spine where the tapes stand out. This last feature is common in ancient bindings in which the bands on the spine were not for decoration - they were caused by the cords that were used for sewing and could not be avoided. These are not elegant bindings, but they can look neat and are very functional.

Prepare the book in the ordinary way, using endpapers with an outside 'waste' sheet, and sew on linen tape to give greater strength. The sewing must be even, and the rounding and backing of a very high order. Clean off the spine with paste, and remember that the leather will show every bump and hollow, so make it really good.

While the book is drying in press - until the next day - make boards from millboard and manilla card. Cut them larger than the finished size, glue two-thirds of the width of each millboard, lay on the manilla cards, and let them dry in press. This will give 'split' boards to hold the tapes. When they are dry, cut them to fit the book, with about the thickness of the board projecting beyond the head and tail, and level at the fore-edge.

Trim the tapes to 1", glue them down to the waste sheet and tear it off ¼" beyond the ends of the tapes.

Now open the split edge of one board and glue the millboard only. Rub the manilla down on it, open it quickly and slide the opening around the flange formed by the tapes and waste sheet, with the manilla toward the book. Don't hold the book by the glued part until the position is right: the squares at head and tail must be equal, and the groove in the joint must be a full ⅛".

Pinch the joint with your fingers, and then attach the other board. Put pressing tins between the boards and the book, and leave the book in press with pressing boards to the groove. The manilla card, being thinner than the millboard, will expand and contract to a greater extent when moistened by glue: this will make the boards concave on the side nearer to the book.

Leather for bookbinding should be flexible, strong, and resistant to decay: all these properties are found in the goatskins that are vegetable-tanned for bookbinding. The undyed colour of the skins is a pinkish buff, so the finished colours cannot be very light or bright. Any white skins, for example, have a cellulose spray finish which resists water - they are difficult to use and should be avoided.

The leather you buy will, almost certainly, be too thick, so each piece that you cut out will need thinning to suit a book. To do this, you will need a spokeshave and a paring knife; a smooth surface will be needed to work on, and an old lithograph stone, a sheet of plate glass with a bevelled and polished edge (an old looking glass), or the marble top of an old wash-stand, will provide this.

The spokeshave

This is a woodworker's tool that works like a plane but has a handle sticking out at each side of the blade. The leather is held in position by leaning against it, or clamping it to the bench, to leave both hands free to use the tool. Whether you use a spokeshave with a flat or a curved sole is unimportant, but the blade should have two adjusting screws, so get the 151 or 0151 model. The opening in the sole is a little narrow, so file away a little of the front edge of the slot; and if it is the flat-soled tool, round the front edge of the sole as well.

The blade must have a razor-sharp edge, and will be more easily ground if you make a holder from a piece of wood with a slot in it to hold the thickness of the blade. Use a coarse stone with paraffin to reduce the angle of the edge to about 10° and curve it slightly. (The drawing is the outline of an actual blade.) When the wafer edge forms, use a fine stone with oil, and then strop the edge to get rid of the burr. When setting the blade in the stock, start with no cutting edge and screw it out gradually until the cut is central.

The paring knife

Make a paring knife from a discarded power hacksaw blade - they are 1″ or 1¼″ wide, and a 14″ or 16″ blade will give two knives better than any you can buy. Grind off the teeth and halve the blade on a power grinder; shape the end and grind the edge as shown overleaf.

The grinding should be ⅜″ wide on a 1¼″ blade - slightly less on a 1″ because the metal is thinner - running from full thickness to nothing at the edge. Try to do a 'hollow grinding', with the ground surface concave. You will know when sufficient nothingness is achieved by the appearance of a fine wafer of steel at the edge. This is the signal to transfer the knife to a coarse stone, with paraffin as a lubricant, then to the fine stone with oil, and then the strop. It's worth taking a lot of trouble to get a good edge, so don't try to hurry it: and, having got it, take care of it. Use your paring knife for no other purpose than paring leather. The drawing, by the way, shows a right-handed knife, so if you need a left-handed one, make a mirror image of it. Both of them must be quite flat on the underside. A useful case to protect the knife can be made by cutting a few strips of millboard wider than the blade, wrapping a piece of paper around them so that the edges overlap and sticking them together with Scotch tape. Then glue brown paper and wind it around, rubbing each layer as it goes down; take out the strips of board and a flat tube will be left. When it is dry, plug one end and keep the knife in it, point first.

Paring leather

Cut leather for the spine cover to project ¾″ beyond the head and tail edges of the board, and wide enough to cover about a quarter of the front and back boards as well as the spine. Fold, but don't crease, the leather, and try to visualise it in the groove between the edge of the board and the joint - try it in the groove if you like - and decide if it will go in easily and flex properly when the book is finished. If it is too thick, it must be thinned with a spokeshave. If the leather is large enough and your bench is the right height, you can hold one end of the leather by leaning against it; if not, a G-clamp with a piece of millboard between the clamp and the leather will hold it to the edge of the bench or the paring stone. Don't use the clamp on glass.

With the leather held in position, flesh side up, you can start to thin it. Hold the spokeshave with both hands and push it along the surface: it will cut more easily if one side is slightly ahead of the other to give a slanting cut. Work systematically all over the surface and check frequently to be sure that there are no local thin spots and, even more frequently, remove any shavings that have slipped under the leather. You will find that fingers are more sensitive to thickness variations than you expected, and by folding the leather and running finger and thumb along the fold, you will quickly notice any variations of thickness. If the end of the leather tends to catch as the spokeshave goes over it, bevel it with the paring knife.

Using a paring-knife.

The second cut.

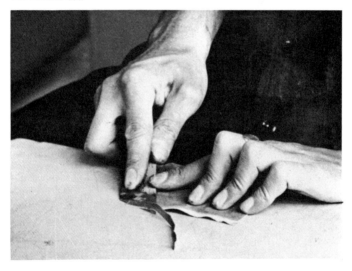

When the leather is thin enough, lay the book on the flesh side and mark the positions of the head and tail edges of the boards. Anything outside the lines will be turned in and will need paring.

Work near the edge of the stone, so that the fingers around the knife are clear of it and the knife can be flat on the stone if necessary.

Hold the leather down with three fingers of the left hand; have the knife edge at 45° to the edge to be pared, and just hold it flat; now, get the four finger-tips of the left hand lined up with the index finger touching the back edge of the knife, press down with three and bend them - the index finger remains straight, pushes the back of the knife and moves it along. If you've kept the knife flat, nothing happens.

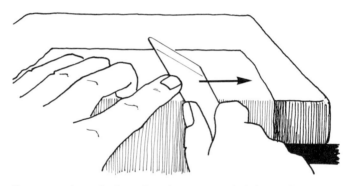

Try again, but tilt the edge down very slightly - it bites into the leather. That's all there is to paring, apart from practice and keeping the edge keen by stropping it frequently - two or three strokes on the bevel, one on the flat, and another on the bevel, will restore the edge: there's no need to press hard, but you must keep the grinding angle or the edge will thicken.

Start near the edge of the turn-in and bevel it about ¼", then work in to make a wider bevel until you reach the line; the turn-in has been pared, but you will need to be sure that the central portion, which is to be doubled over on itself and stuck to the spine, will not cause a bump to appear on the spine of the book. Turn the leather right side up with the turn-in folded under, and feel for bumps. If you find any, you must do more paring: if not, you've won.

Pare both turn-ins and then, using the point of the knife, edge-pare the two long edges - but no more than ¼″ wide.

A book with a leather back only is called quarter-bound. If you decide to make a half-binding, corners are needed or, if the five-sided shape of the sides is not to your liking, you can have leather strips along the fore-edge of the boards - they look pleasant and protect the edges.

Cut the shape of a corner from some thin board and use it as a pattern for cutting the leather, but if any spokeshaving is necessary, do that before cutting out. Pare the long and short edges of each corner, holding the knife at an angle of about 30°, with one cut going right through the leather

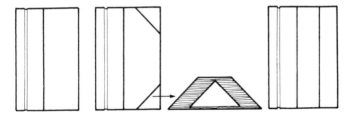

- there must be no fluffy edge. The remaining two sides must be pared in the same way as the turn-in at head and tail. The only part not pared will be the triangle that shows on the outside, and that should be the same thickness as the leather on the spine. When paring strips for the fore-edge, there will be three edges to pare for turning in, and the remaining one can be edge-pared.

Covering with leather

This is a leisurely affair because paste is used and it dries slowly. It is useful to know, before you start, that contact with iron will make black stains on damp leather, so don't have any steel tools on the bench if you can avoid doing so, and keep them well out of the way if you can't. The paste brush should be string-bound or aluminium-ferruled.

Paste the leather corners (or the fore-edge strips) well but thinly, using firm brush strokes, and leave them with the pasted surfaces face to face to become tacky. While this is happening, make a protective 'cap' for the edges of the book - a sheet of paper, larger than the book, laid inside the back board and, with the front board open, wrapped tightly over the head and tail and fastened over the front endpaper with Scotch tape. The width should be sufficient to overlap the fore-edge by about ½". This is to guard against getting paste on the edges of the book.

Lay the leather on the boards in approximately correct positions; open the boards and adjust the leather so that only the parts to be turned in are showing. Put the outside of one board down on the stone, hold it there with the book resting on your hand, and use the pointed end of a folder to lift the turn-in and set the leather against the edge of the board. Turn in one edge, tuck in the corner with a spot of paste on the tucked-in part, and then turn in the other edge. This should make an invisible joint: if, however, there is a ridge or hollow where the edges lap, you will find that leather will stand a lot of pushing around, so aim to get the perfect joint. If you are turning in fore-edge strips, cut off the corners in much the same way as you would with cloth, but with the point of the paring knife held at an angle of 30° - and put some paste on the cut edge before turning in.

Now for the spine. Paste the leather in the same way as you did the corners, then bend it over on itself without making a crease; this traps the moisture which can only get out through the skin. If you cover two books at once, paste both covers and put them face to face. Leave them for about ten minutes. During this time, find a piece of string of the same thickness as the boards and work paste into the fibres - you only need about 4" if the book is not a thick one. Open up the leather and paste it once more; close it again and leave it to become tacky. If, by pressing the pasted surface with your finger, you can pick up the leather, it is ready to put on the book. While this condition is developing, cut two pieces of the pasted string to put inside the turn-in at the head and tail - they should be the same length as the thickness of the book and boards. Also clean the stone or glass on which you will work, get rid of any leather shavings, clean a pointed folder, and have a damp sponge ready for when you need it. The turn-in of the leather will go between the book and the boards, so cut the waste sheet where it goes into the split of the boards - but no farther than the tape.

Paste slightly the spine, the joint and an inch of the boards, to keep the porous surfaces from drawing the moisture from the pasted leather; open the leather and lay it, paste side up, on the stone. Place the spine of the book on the leather in a central position and lift; if the paste has the right tackiness, the leather will be picked up by the book. Stand the book on its fore-edge and gently but firmly, without stretching the leather, use the palms of your hands to draw the cover down on the boards and, still with your palm, rub along the spine.

Lay the book on one side, lift the leather as far as the joint, press it into the groove with the bone folder, and put the leather down with the side of your hand; then do the same on the other side. Well set joints ensure a good opening of the boards. Put the short pieces of string on the pasted leather, so that they lie curved along the head and tail of the book, and cover the turn-in at one end with a piece of waxed paper so that you can stand the book on that end without getting paste on its edge.

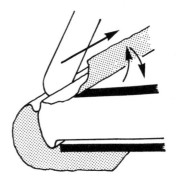

With the book on end, and its spine away from you, put a smear of paste on the outside of the central portion of the turn-in above the spine - this will help it to stick to the book when it is turned in.

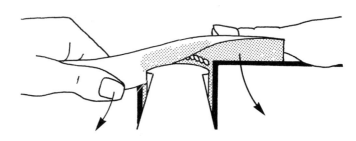

Open the boards, place your index and middle fingers about 2″ down the spine, rest the centres of your palms on the edges of the boards and use your thumbs to draw the turn-in over the edge of the boards and down inside. With any luck, the pieces of string will stay in position to thicken the leather over the head and tail. If, when you close the book, the ridge is on the spine, you must put it right at once - it may be necessary to open out and start again, but the string must be in its proper place. Stretch the leather down inside the boards with your thumbs, turn the book over, remove the waxed paper and turn in the other end. Use a folder to set the leather in the joints again, then make a slip knot from smooth string and tie the book with the string lying in the joint and the knot at the head or tail: Scotch tape the end to the paper protecting the edge to keep it out of the way.

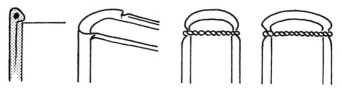

Stand the book on end again. The leather is pulled in by the slipknot, so use the point of a folder to push out the leather on each side of the string until the boards are straight and the 'head cap' as wide as the rest of the book. Hold the book firmly and rub down the leather on the spine with the palm of your hand; turn the book over, grip it with both hands, and roll the head and tail on the stone to make the

Cut-out patterns of thick paper were glued to the boards before the cases were made to make these decorations.

A case made from strips of coloured cloth and paper.

Careful work with drawing instruments produced this.

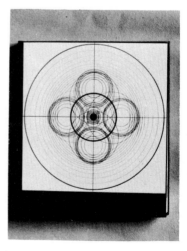

A knife was the only tool used in the decoration of these books - apart from the lettering.

Bob Akers using a fillet to run lines in gold.

string lie over the book instead of causing a bump at each end. Wash off any paste marks with a damp sponge, slip a sheet of waxed paper inside each board to prevent moisture penetration, and put the book between two clean boards to dry. Before you leave it with a weight on the top board, look to see that nothing is twisted. Remove the string when the leather is dry.

Siding

Cloth or paper sides will be thinner than leather, so the level of the boards must be raised to give a neater finish. This is called 'filling in'.

To get the positions of the dotted lines in the drawing, set your spring dividers to a quarter of the board width and mark both ends of the spine cover; increase the setting by a half to make marks on the corners. Lay a rule to the marks, and run a pointed folder along it to make grooves.

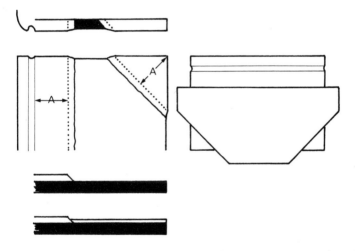

Use a knife to bevel the leather without cutting away the line, and remove the strips. Where the corners go over the edge of the board, they should be trimmed at 45° - not square - so that there will be no gap when the sides go on.

Cut a piece of manilla card to fit with its edges half-way up the bevels that you have cut, but let it hang over the edges of the boards. Glue the manilla, lay it on the board, rub down with the edge of a folder, and trim off the projecting edges with a pair of shears.

Make cloth sides by laying the straight edge of a piece of cloth on the line marked on the spine cover, holding it in position and folding back to the lines marked on the corners. Put the cloth on a zinc plate and use a knife and straight-edge to cut through the folds. This should fit the side on which it was marked, so slip it inside the board while you cut the other side. Trim the turn-in of the cloth to about $\frac{3}{4}''$; glue the side, lay it to the marks on the leather, and turn in. If you are doing a quarter binding, there are no corners to bother with and putting on the sides is even simpler than making a cloth case.

Mark an even margin on the inside of each board with your dividers, and trim it round with a sharp knife held at an angle to produce a bevel. After removing the offcuts, paste down the endpapers and give the book a light nip in press before opening it. Remove the paper cap, put in pressing tins with paper folded over them, and leave the book in press to dry with pressing boards laid to the groove.

This is a very good binding for music scores, as it opens quite flat; but the rounding and backing should be kept very small to suit the thin boards desirable on work of this kind.

Gold finishing

When a book is bound in leather, the time has come to try your hand at using gold leaf. This gives a cleaner look to the letters and has less of the glitter that is usual when foil is used, but you can use gold foil if you wish.

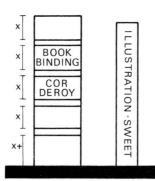

Before lettering the spine, tool a blind line on each side of the raised bands caused by the tapes, but be sure that they are all the same width and equally spaced by marking them with dividers. If the lettering is to run down the spine, you must ignore the tapes and leave the spine free for lettering.

Make a pattern of the lettering on thin paper and 'fix it in position on the book with small pieces of Scotch tape; use warm tools to blind in the impressions and take off the pattern. If you think the lettering is not clear, go over it without the pattern, but don't make deep impressions or the gold will break when you lay it on.

Prepare the leather by washing it with a little vinegar if it is goatskin; porous leathers, such as calf and sheep, need washing with thin paste to fill the pores. If you do paste-wash, dab the surface all over with the side of your hand to avoid streakiness.

Paint in the impressions with a glair made from the white of an egg with a teaspoon of vinegar beaten into it. Leave it to stand overnight and then strain it through fine cotton wool or several thicknesses of fine cloth. Let the glair dry before giving it a second coat. Glair is sometimes used on cloth, but is applied with a sponge. There are many prescriptions for making glair - you may find others you like better, but this one is basic.

Gold leaf is very thin and weak: it is also nearly free of any other metals - about 23 carat. The knife and gold cushion must be free of grease, and you mustn't touch the leaf with your fingers. In a draught-free room, lay the gold-book on the cushion and use your left hand to lift the edge that opens; let the cover and end leaves fall until the lowest leaf of gold is exposed; open the book a little more, slide the gold knife under the leaf, open the book completely, and slide the gold to the surface of the cushion. Remove the book, withdraw the knife, and blow lightly at the centre of the leaf from a distance of about 3″ - don't breathe on it, just a slight puff will flatten it. Cut the leaf to useful sizes, and lay a small box over the cushion to keep out air currents.

Use a small piece of cotton wool to apply the merest trace of vaseline to the spine - you should be unable to feel that it is greasy. Keep the greasy pad away from the gold book, knife, and cushion.

With a larger piece of cotton wool - about the area of your hand - make a gold pad: fold in two sides of the cotton wool and bend it in half to give a squarish corner. Hold it in your hand with the index finger straight and on one corner of the pad. Passing the pad lightly over your hair will make it greasy enough to pick up the gold leaf, so do this and press down firmly on one of the cut pieces of gold: it should

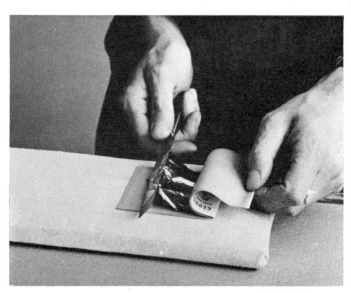

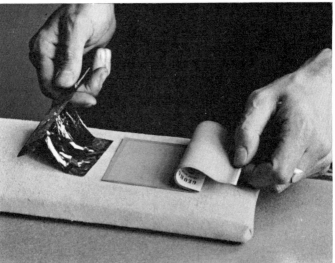

Handling gold leaf.

stay on the pad so that you can transfer it to the more greasy leather. Press it down firmly and without any rubbing motion, and it will stay on the leather with every variation of texture and the impressions showing clearly; if the blinding of the lettering was too deep, the gold will have to stretch too much and may break. If this happens, lay on another layer of gold with no preparation - it will usually stick, but if you breathe on the book before doing it, there will be no doubt about it.

All that needs doing now is to press hot tools in the previously prepared impressions, clean away the surplus gold with a gold rubber, and admire the results.

The traditional test for a hot tool is to touch it with a licked finger: if it remains wet, the tool isn't hot yet; if it evaporates immediately, it is too hot and may burn the leather; if a spot of moisture gradually boils away, it should be about right - but you'd better try for yourself on a piece of leather stuck to some millboard.

A quick, firm, but not heavy, impression of the tool should be your aim: the fingers of your hand around the tool-handle, the thumb on top, and the thumb-nail of the other hand to steady the hot end as you strike the tool.

Experienced finishers can deal with the hot end without pain, but you will find it more comfortable to have a small piece of leather - about half the size of a typewriter key - glued to the part of your thumb that needs protection. Don't disdain this - it will help you to get better results.

Fault finder

Gold does not stick	Cold tools; leather too dry; book glaired for too long; not enough glair (one coat).
Gold sticks around edges of impression	Tools too hot, or held in impression for too long a time; leather too moist; glair not dry.
Tool goes through leather	Tool too hot; leather wet; both of these.
Letters dull	Tools dirty - polish them on a piece of leather; tools too hot.

The late Mr Joseph Zaehnsdorf devoted forty-seven pages of his book to the subject of finishing, so a lot remains unsaid on the subject in this book. You may find that laying on two layers of gold will give better results; it is not necessary to re-glair when a letter needs re-tooling, unless it is obstinate; another coat of glair, being fresh, will often do the trick. Poor results are often due to the glair not being freshly applied.

You will learn about gold leaf by using it - there is no standard treatment, and every finisher develops his own methods. They all agree that clean tools are essential.

12 Decoration

Up to now, this book has been about the stark realities of bookbinding. There is a lighter side: decoration is not a necessity, but most of us prefer some mark of individuality on our work and like it to look attractive. You, as a binder, are in a position to make something different from all the others, and the cost of production need only be measured against your satisfaction.

Traditional methods of decoration need not be more complicated than the lettering of a book. Simple tools can be combined to make pleasing patterns: they are cheap to buy and easy to make.

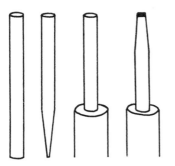

If you want to make them, you will need a small vice, some files, a drill and some twist drill bits, and one of those little saws that will cut metal. Never hold anything that the vice can hold better.

Start with a 4″ length of round or square brass rod about the thickness of a pencil. File one end to a rough point and fix it in a hole drilled in one end of a 6″ length of ¾″ dowel.

File the brass to the shape you want - a small square, for example - but remember that you will need to see along the tool, so make a long taper to the edge of the shape. Finish the face of the tool with fine emery, and polish with chalk or jeweller's rouge on a piece of leather. A slight curvature of the face will make the impressions reflect light from more directions and look brighter.

Try a simple pattern. Cut some thin paper (30 gsm) to the size of one board of a book; divide the short side in five equal parts, the long side in seven, then join the marks to make a lozenge pattern. Fasten the pattern, over some gold foil, to the book cover; tool in the dots where the lines cross - but you must keep the tool hot enough to make the gold stick. If you fasten the pattern at the four corners with Scotch tape, you will be able to check the work without disturbing its position.

This basic principle of working on a grid pattern can be very useful; numerous variations are possible, producing controlled, pleasing layouts. One student made a blind-tooled repeat pattern by pressing fishhooks into the cover.

You need not stick to a plain square - it can be made more interesting by cutting it in four with a saw. Many shapes can be made with files and a saw; and if you drill a hole in the brass and file around it, you will make a circle - but the hole comes first.

There are many colours of cloth on which gold doesn't show up well, so try other coloured foils on them. You may find that these foils require more heat than gold to make them stick.

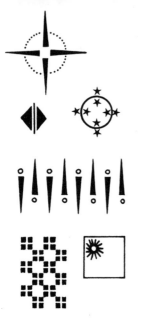

If you want to make long straight lines or gentle curves, you will need a fillet. These can be bought, but it's much more satisfying to trade the binding of a book to the enthusiastic owner of a lathe.

For straight lines, a large wheel is the easiest to use - over 3″ diameter if possible. For curved lines, 'farthing fillets' made from small coins have been used, but they don't hold the heat well: small fillets made from thick brass give more satisfaction.

A separate wheel is needed for each thickness of line but, if you don't want to use them all at once, they can be made interchangeable on one tang. The centres would have to be identical to allow the same screw to fit all of them. This has been done, but the usefulness of the idea depends very much upon the use that the tools will have made of them.

This drawing of a fillet shows the constructional details. The bronze wheel should run freely, but without side play, on the steel screw; the tang, also of steel, should be set three or four inches into the handle of 1¼″ dowel, 12″ long. There should be no more than six inches of the tool pro-

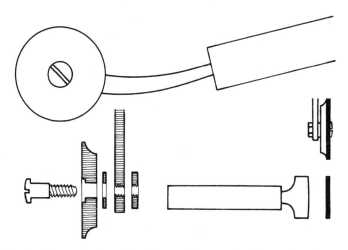

jecting from the handle. Those fillets and rolls in the Jost Amman woodcut would be impossible to use. Each fillet should have a short pallet - a one-line tool - to match it: this is used to finish lines neatly. The edges of fillets and pallets must be highly polished, so protect them when they are not in use.

A great deal of decoration can be done with nothing more complicated than a sharp knife with a fine point, and the results can be very attractive. Except for the titles, only a knife was used to do the work on the books shown in the colour illustration on p. 36 of this book. You can have relief patterns, variations in texture, and areas of different colour, that would not be available on any but the most expensive bindings. These patterns need clean, neat work and planning, but the results are worth it. Try making a case with vertical strips of cloth or, if you like, cloth and paper. They need not all be the same width, or straight, or parallel, but for mechanical reasons the spine and joints should be in one piece. If the strips are all the same thickness and unlikely to fray, the edges can be butted (laid edge to edge); but if some may fray, overlap them with others that will not.

Relief patterns must be built up on the board before the covering is done. Simple shapes, giving a raised pattern that shows through the covering material, can often transform what might have been a dull cover into one of considerable interest.

Cut rectangles of thin card - they need not be the same size, and odd numbers combine better - and glue them to the board after you have decided how to arrange them; then make the case in the ordinary way. Press it, before the glue is dry, with a packing of several sheets of blotting paper over the patterned board.

If you cut holes in a card, glue it to a board and trim it to fit the book, the pattern will be recessed: but you must line the inside of the board with pasted paper to counteract the pull of the card when it shrinks as the moisture dries out. Remember the grain direction. In the recessed areas, it will be safe to put panels of different coloured cloth or paper: the edges of the onlay will be protected. Experiment with this method and remember that bold, simple shapes give the best results.

Inlaid decoration is possible. Line the boards with paper, on both sides, before making the case. When it is made, use rubber solution to stick a piece of different material on the front cover and, over that, some paper with the pattern drawn on it. Try some large simple outline letters for a start.

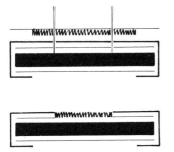

When the rubber solution has set, use a knife with a thin sharp point to cut around the letters, through the paper and both thicknesses of cloth; peel down to the original cover, remove the cut out letters (the paper lining of the boards will split) and stick the inlay in its place with glue. The paper and rubber solution can be rubbed away when the glue has dried.

If the material of the cover has a coarse weave, you may find it necessary to fix the fibres with a clear cellulose spray before applying rubber solution which may penetrate too deeply to come away easily.

If all you need to get a desired effect is a patch of colour, the simplest way to get it is to use Letrafilm - a thin, self-adhesive, coloured plastic film that can be cut with scissors or a knife to the shape you want, peeled from its backing, laid in position, and rubbed down. Before you decide on it, make a trial on the material of the cover to find if it will come away too easily. You may find that a cellulose spray will fix the edges, or you may have to cover it with a transparent self-adhesive film that can be turned in over the edges of the board. There are many points in favour of the inlay method - it uses scraps that would have been thrown out.

Lettering is decorative if it is well-formed and properly spaced; and the letter-transfer sheets that are available are so easy to use that you should do so. Look at new buildings with lettering on them - many banks and shops provide good examples of the effective use of lettering - and notice that there is space between the letters, not a distance. Keep the gap between words to the minimum needed to separate them. You'll soon learn to recognise a good piece of lettering.

13   Repairing cloth covers

The complete rebinding of a worn book may be a wrong solution to the problem of preservation: many book-lovers like to keep them in their familiar covers, some of which have a lot to commend them. Many nineteenth-century books were masterpieces in their way - the decoration would be too much for modern books, but it was right then.

Scotch tape is not the answer, but it can be removed with carbon tetrachloride (Carbona) along with the dirt that it has collected. The cover is broken at the joints and so are the endpapers, but the mull and tape hold them together.

Make shallow cuts around the tapes, through the endpapers, and lift the tapes. Cut the mull along the joints and the book should come away from its case. If the book-sewing is still good, there is no need to re-sew; but it may be necessary to pull the book, do some repairs, re-sew through the same holes if possible, tip on new endpapers, and follow the whole procedure of glueing, rounding, backing, and lining with mull and paper. If you re-sew, be very careful to keep the sections level - the old cover will be used again and the edges will not be cut.

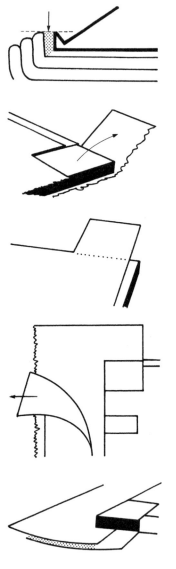

New endpapers on a book
that is not to be re-sewn
must be tipped on so that the
folded edges fit right into the
joint - the fold must be level
with the back fold of the section
if there is to be no strain on it.
Remove the old back linings
by putting the book between
pressing boards in the lying-press
and cleaning off with paste.
Leave the book to dry,
and then re-line it.

Now for the case. The joint
of the front board is broken
but the turn-in is still holding,
so cut that to free the board.
Cut through the turn-in about
an inch from the joint and lift it,
then do the same at the other end;
turn over the board and lift
the cloth from it along the whole
back edge to a depth of about
an inch. Put a zinc plate between
the board and the cloth
and cut off the rough edge
so that it falls a little short
of the edge of the board.
If the joint of the back board
has gone, give it the same
treatment: if it is still intact,
lift the turn-in from the spine
and an inch of the back board,
and cut the frayed edge to make
it tidy. Remove the stiffener
from the spine.

Cut a piece of bookcloth (the
same colour as the case)
wide enough to reach across
the spine and ½″ of each board,
with a narrow turn-in at the ends.
Glue the outside of the new
cloth to the underside of the old,

so that ½″ will be between the old cover and the board; then insert the rest of the glued part inside the detached front board. Be certain that the cover will fit before rubbing down. Use a piece of stiff paper longer than the boards to put glue between the boards and the cover - glue an inch wide along the paper, slip it between the board and the cloth, press down with your hand and pull out the paper. The glue will transfer to the board, and it will stick to the cloth.

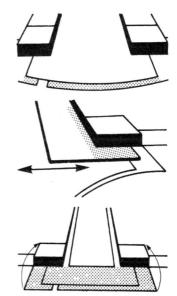

Cut out and glue in a new stiffener, glue the cloth at the head and tail, turn it in, and the case is repaired.

If both boards have broken joints, all that is necessary is to lift the cloth from their back edges, cut a new stiffener for the spine, glue the cloth on the underside and use it to join the boards and make a case to fit the book. The rough edges at the joint must still be trimmed back so that they will not be in a part of the case where they will be expected to bend. If the edges of the old cloth are stuck to well supported new material, they will stay down; if they flex, they will come away. Glue on the old spine.

When the cover is completed, give it a wash with a sponge damped in glue and water. Don't rub hard or the colour will shift, and try to avoid wetting the gold blocking. This treatment removes some dirty marks and revives the cloth.

This is a worth-while activity if you are interested in preserving records. The early bookbinders' cases are disappearing and, too late, it has been found that they have merit and the skills that were employed to make them will never return.

This book has no space for leather repairs, but the principles are the same, except that boards must be left on if cords still hold them. The spine, after being cleaned off with paste, would need a new hollow-back lining; the old leather, probably tender, would need more delicate handling than cloth, and the repair leather would have to be pared so that no bumps formed anywhere.

List of suppliers

H. Band & Co. Ltd, Plough Yard, High St, Brentford, Middx: leather and vellum (sample card).

Gilbert Bingham & Son Ltd, 188 Iverson Rd, London, N.W. 6: blocking foil and information.

J. Hewit & Sons Ltd, 125 High St, Edinburgh, and 89 St John St, London, E.C.1: professional scale equipment; hand tools for bookbinding; leather; cut lengths of cloth; all bookbinding materials.

Jackson's Board Mills Ltd, Bourne End, Bucks: millboards in 56 lb bundles. .

H. Kelly & Sons, 252 Goswell Road, London, E.C.1: typeholders.

T. N. Lawrence & Sons, 2 Bleeding Heart Yard, Greville St, London, E.C.1: paper by the sheet; hand and machine-made papers; imported papers including Japanese tissue.

T. Mackrell & Co. Ltd, Witham, Essex: hand letters to specification, decorative finishing tools.

Le Meuble d'Imprimerie, 132 rue Boucicaut, Fontenay-aux-Roses, Seine, France: all amateur and professional equipment.

Revertex Ltd, Harlow, Essex: Emultex K.515, PVC adhesive.

Russell Bookcrafts, Hitchin, Herts: amateur equipment and tools; Digby Stuart Press; leather; paper and boards in small quantities; Postlip laminating tissue.

Taylor & Co. (Tools) Ltd, 54 Old St, London, E.C.1: punching tools; press studs, eyelets, rivets plus tools.

George M. Whiley Ltd, Victoria Rd, Ruislip, Middx: blocking foil and gold leaf (sample card); hand letters and type, typeholders (catalogue).

U.S. suppliers

Andrews-Nelson-Whitehead Inc., 7 Laight St, New York 19: leather; parchment; decorative papers; art papers from the orient; cover papers, lining papers and mending paper.

Carter, Rice, Storrs & Bement, 273 Summer St, Boston, Mass.: Strathmore printing and speciality papers; text and cover papers.

W. O. Hickok Manufacturing Co., Ninth and Cumberland Sts, Harrisburg, Penn.: professional equipment and small tools.

Craftools Inc., 396 Broadway, New York 13: tools; needles and threads; binders' boards; paste.

A. I. Friedman, 25 West 45th St, New York 36: brushes, knives; pastes, glue, varnishes; boards and cover papers.

Ernest Schaefer C., 74-8 Oraton St, Newark 4, New Jersey: bone folders, plow knives, plastic foils.

Technical Library Service, 261 Broadway, New York: presses; folders; cloth; glair; leather protector and dressing.

Henry Westphal & Co., 4 East 32nd St, New York: knives; folders; files; rabbit-ear hammers for corners.

For further reading

Pictorial Manual of Bookbinding by Manly Banister. The Ronald Press, New York, 1958.

Bookbinding and the care of books by D. Cockerell. Pitman, London, 1955.

Marbling as a school subject by S. Cockerell. Russell, Hitchin, 1934.

Bookcrafts for senior pupils by A. F. Collins. Dryad. London, 1949.

Creative Bookbinding by Pauline Johnson. University of Washington Press, Washington, 1963.

Basic Bookbinding by A. W. Lewis, Batsford. London, 1952; Dover Publications, New York, 1957.

Simple bookbinding for junior schools by W. F. Matthews. Pitman, London, 1930.

Foil tooling by J. Mason. Russell, Hitchin.

Bookbinding by hand by L. Town. Faber & Faber, London, 1951.

Modern Bookbinding by A. J. Vaughan, Skilton, London, 1960.

Hand Bookbinding: a manual of instruction by Aldren A. Watson. Reinhold, New York, 1963.

The Art of Bookbinding by J. Zaehnsdorf. Bell, London, 1880.

Index

Backing   47, 48, 77
Board cutting   15, 16, 50
Boards, backing   9, 42, 47
   press   9, 20, 37, 53, 61, 65
Bookcloth   25, 68, 100
Brush, glue   9, 24, 42, 50

Cambric   41, 66, 67
CTC   26, 99
Casemaking   50, 51-55
Casing-in   53
Cellulose spray   26, 59, 99
Cleaning off spine   48, 77
Collating   60
Cutting clamp   16, 19, 45, 50

Decoration   36, 69, 87-8, 96-9

Edge-cutting   43-5, 66-8, 71
Endpapers   41-2, 53, 66-8, 77,
   100

Fillets   88, 96-7
Finishing   55-6, 58-9, 91-4
Finishing faults   93
Folding   37-8, 49

Glair   26, 91, 94
Glue   26, 42, 50
Gluing   42, 49
Gluing cloth   50, 52
Gold leaf   90-94
Gold rubber   27
G.s.m.   28
Guards   61-2, 64, 71

Hand-letters   55-57

Kettle-stitch   40, 72
Knife   7, 10, 78-80, 82-3

Leather   27, 77-8, 80-83
Leather covering   81, 84-6, 89
Lettering   52, 59, 69, 91, 99
Letter-spacing   56, 58-59
Letraset, etc.   59, 69, 98
Library binding   77-86, 89-94

Lying-press or substitute   13, 14,
   18, 22, 37, 43, 47-8, 50, 66-7

Machine direction   30, 37, 42,
   48, 50, 62, 64, 71, 73, 75
Marking for sewing   38, 62
Mull   28, 42, 48

Overcasting   72

Paper   28, 30-33
Paring leather   80-83
Paste   28, 53, 64, 71
Photograph album   75-6
Plough   13-4, 18, 35, 43-4
Pressing   38, 53, 61-2, 68, 77
Pulling   60, 61

Rebinding books   60-64
Repairing cases   99-101
Repairing paper   63-4
Round corners   54-5
Rounding   46, 77

Sections   37-42, 60-62, 71
Sequence of operations   34
Sewing   35, 38-40, 42, 62, 72, 77
   frame and keys   13, 21, 39
   unsewn books   71-76
   side   73-76
Sharpening knives   79-80
Siding   89-90
Signatures   60
Spine   45-9, 65-68, 77
Split boards   77-8
Spokeshave   70, 78-80
'Swell'   39, 46-7, 71-2

Thread   29, 37, 39, 66-7
Type   56-9
Type-clamp   24, 58-9
Type-holder   56-8

Universal corners   54
Unsewn binding   65-8

Weaver's knot   40